T0163247

Everyday
Malay Phrase Book
& Dictionary

by Thomas G. Oey
revised by Sharifah Zahrah Alwee Alkadri

PERIPLUS EDITIONS
Singapore • Hong Kong • Indonesia

Published by Periplus Editions (HK) Ltd.

www.periplus.com

Copyright © 2004 Periplus Editions (HK) Ltd.

LCC Card No. 94065389
ISBN 978-962-593-533-1

Distributors

North America, Latin America & Europe
Tuttle Publishing
364 Innovation Drive
North Clarendon, VT 05759-9436, USA
Tel: 1 (802) 773 8930; Fax: 1 (802) 773 6993
info@tuttlepublishing.com
www.tuttlepublishing.com

Japan
Tuttle Publishing
Yaekari Building 3rd Floor, 5-4-12 Osaki
Shinagawa-ku, Tokyo 1410032, Japan
Tel: (81) 3 5437 0171; Fax: (81) 3 5437 0755
sales@tuttle.co.jp
www.tuttle.co.jp

Asia Pacific
Berkeley Books Pte Ltd
3 Kallang Sector #04-01
Singapore 349278
Tel: (65) 6741 2178; Fax: (65) 6741 2179
inquiries@periplus.com.sg
www.tuttlepublishing.com

Indonesia
PT Java Books Indonesia
Jl. Rawa Gelam IV No. 9
Kawasan Industri Pulogadung
Jakarta 13930, Indonesia
Tel: 62 (21) 4682 1088; Fax: 62 (21) 461 0206
crm@periplus.co.id
www.periplus.com

Printed in Malaysia

27 26 25 24   15 14 13 12   2402VP

Contents

Introduction

Bahasa Malaysia (literally "the Malaysian language"), is based on Malay which is the mother tongue of the Malays of the Peninsula and the people of central eastern Sumatra. Malay is an Austronesian language (Malayo-Polynesian) that is closely related to languages throughout Indonesia, the Philippines and the Pacific Islands, and it has been for centuries the lingua franca of Southeast Asia.

Malaysia today is a culturally diverse country, with Malays, Chinese, Indians, Proto-Malay or Orang Asli people, and at least fifty different ethnic groups living in the Borneo states of Sabah and Sarawak. Bahasa Malaysia, while being based on Malay, has incorporated words from many of the different languages spoken in the country, as well as words from Arabic, Sanskrit, Portuguese and English.

In line with the Malaysian government's policy of developing a truly national language, foreign words incorporated into Bahasa Malaysia are spelled as they are pronounced by Malays. Thus, many English words are not immediately recognizable, but if they are pronounced according to the following pronunciation guide, their meaning becomes clear. *Teksi, basikal, farmasi* and *akitek* are just some of these "Malaysianized" words.

It is important to realize that for many Malaysians, the national language (which they often refer to by its initials, BM) is not their mother tongue and their pronunciation and degree of proficiency in the language vary. Although English is widely spoken in the towns, you will find when in rural areas that speaking Malay is an enormous help. Even if they speak English, Malaysians are invariably delighted when foreigners attempt to speak their national language, and tell you how *pandai* (clever) you are even when you utter just a few simple words.

The lessons in this book are prioritized, with more important words and phrases being given first, so that you may profit no matter how deeply into the book you go. By studying the first section only, you acquire a basic "survival" Bahasa Malaysia, and by mastering the first three sections you should be able to get around quite well on your own. In order to present each lesson clearly as a unit, we have found it necessary in some cases to repeat vocabulary.

Colloquial Malay, which is the most commonly spoken and the most readily understood form of the language, is used here rather than "formal" BM. Care has been taken to include only vocabulary that has immediate practical application for visitors. By repetition and memorization of the materials, you will quickly gain a grasp of the language's basic elements. Rather than include long and tedious lists of words and phrases in the lessons themselves, we have appended at the back of the book a miniature bilingual dictionary that should be adequate for the needs of most tourists.

At the end of the book you will also find additional information on the use of verb and noun affixes, and suggestions for further study. Do not be deceived by the claim that "Malay has no grammar". As one studies the language in greater depth, one realizes how complex it actually is. After several months or years, you may realize that while you are able to speak the language *secukupnya* (sufficiently), it is as difficult as any other language to truly master. In fact, the grammar, morphology and syntax of standard Bahasa Malaysia as taught in the schools is at least as complex as any European language.

Thomas G. Oey
and Sharifah Zahrah Alwee Alkadri

Selamat Datang!

The Basics

Pronunciation

To learn to pronounce the language correctly, it is best to ask a native speaker to read aloud some of the examples given in this section, then try to imitate his or her pronunciation. Be aware, however, that there are a number of variations in accent within Malaysia. The accent in Johor (and among Singapore's Malays) is very different to that of the people of Kelantan, near the Thai border. Many of the people in the Borneo states of Sabah and Sarawak speak with an accent closer to that of Indonesia. They also incorporate many Indonesian words into the language. However, the stress on words is generally placed on the second to last syllable.

Unlike English, the spelling of Bahasa Malaysia is consistently phonetic. Many consider that the pronunciation is similar to Spanish or Italian.

Consonants

Most are pronounced roughly as in English. The main exceptions are as follows:

c is pronounced "ch" (formerly spelled "ch").

    cari to look for, seek   *cinta* to love

g is always hard, as in "girl."

    guna to use   *gila* crazy

h is very soft, and often not pronounced.

    habis (*abis*) finished   *hidup* (*idup*) to live

This is the case only when the word begins with the letter "h," and not if the "h" is in between or at the end of the word. For example:

lihat (pronounced as *lihat*) to see

Without "h" (**liat**) it means "tough."

mudah (pronounced as *mudah*) easy   **muda** – young

sudah (pronounced as *sudah*) already

However, **tahu** (to know) is an exception as it can be pronounced as *tau*.

kh is found in words of Arabic derivation, and sounds like a hard "k."

khabar news   **khusus** special

ng is always soft, as in "hanger."

dengar to hear   **hilang** lost

ngg is always hard, as in "hunger."

ganggu to bother   **mangga** mango

r   is trilled or rolled, as in Spanish.

ratus hundred   **baru** new

Vowels

As in English, there are five written vowels (a, e, i, o, u) and two diphthongs (ai, au).

a   is very short, like the "a" in "father."

satu one   **bayar** to pay

e   is usually unaccented, like the "u" in "but."

empat four   **beli** to buy

When stressed, however, *e* sounds like the "é" in "passé."

désa village   **bébas** free

i   is long like the "ea" in "bean."

    tiga three   **lima** five

o   is long, as in "so."

    bodoh stupid   **boleh** can, may

u   is long like the "u" in "humour."

    tujuh seven   **untuk** for

au   is like the "ow" in "how."

    atau or   **pulau** island

ai   is pronounced like the word "eye."

    pantai beach   **sampai** to reach

Note: Many Malaysians in the central states of Penin-su-lar Malaysia, especially around Kuala Lumpur, tend to narrow the final "a" sound, making it almost like an "er." Thus, **ada** sounds more like *ader*. The people of Kelantan are reputed to drag out the diphthong "ai," so that **air** sounds more like *aiyor*.

Selamat pagi.

Greetings

Greetings in Malaysia vary with ethnic group and the degree of Westernization. Many Malaysians will shake hands in the Western fashion. Muslims often touch the right hand to their heart after a gentle hand clasp. Kissing and other physical greetings are sometimes practised by the more sophisticated Malaysians in the cities, but not in rural areas or among conservative Muslims.

Selamat is a word used in most Malaysian greetings. It comes from the Arabic **salam**, meaning "peace," "safety" or "salvation." By itself, **Selamat!** means "Well being" (safe), such as in **Selamat jalan** (safe journey; bon voyage). Like the English "good," it is followed by the time of day and other words to form most common greetings.

Selamat datang	Welcome (*datang* = to come)
Selamat pagi	Good morning (*pagi* = morning, until 11 am)
Selamat tengah hari	Good day (*tengah hari* = midday, from 12 pm to 2 pm)
Selamat petang	Good afternoon (*petang* = late afternoon, 3 pm to 7 pm)
Selamat malam	Good evening (*malam* = night, after dark) and Good night

Apa khabar is another common greeting which literally means "What's the news?" (**apa** = what, **khabar** = news) or, in other words, "How are you?" The standard answer is **Khabar baik**, meaning "I'm fine" (**baik** = well, fine). The colloquial **Apa macam?** (literally "What kind") is sometimes used in place of **Apa khabar** among friends.

You will also find yourself greeted with the following questions, even by complete strangers.

Mau/Nak ke mana? Where are you going?
(lit: Want-to-where?)

Mau for **mahu** is generally used by the non-Malays in Malaysia when talking to a Malay. Malays generally use *nak* for **hendak**.

Dari mana?	Where are you [coming] from?
(lit: From-where?)	

This is said out of courtesy, and the person is usually not all that interested in your movements.

You may answer:

Dari [+ place]	From [+ place]
Saya mau/nak ke [+ place]	I am going to [+ place]
Jalan-jalan saja.	Just going for a walk.
(lit: Walk-walk-only.)	
Makan angin.	Travelling
(lit: Eat-wind.)	

This is generally used when visiting or on tour.

Bersiar-siar.	Just out for some air.
(lit: Take-a-walk.)	
Tidak ke mana-mana.	Not anywhere in particular.
(lit: Not-to-where-where.)	

When taking leave of someone, it is polite to excuse oneself by saying:

Maaf, saya pergi dulu.	Excuse me. I am going now.
(lit: Excuse, I-go-first.)	(= Goodbye for now!)
Jumpa lagi.	See you again.
(lit: Meet-again.)	

More informally, you can also use the widely understood:

Bye-Bye!	Goodbye! (So long!)

If you are the one staying behind, you respond by saying:

Selamat jalan.	Bon voyage.
(lit: Safe-journey.)	

Forms of Address

There are many ways of addressing someone in Malaysia. Because of their innate politeness and sense of respect when addressing people of different social status, Malays use forms of address that carry certain distinctions. Certain forms of address which are "safe" in a wide variety of situations should be learned first and used most often.

Encik is the most common way of addressing an adult male, in much the same way as Mr or Sir is used in English.

Puan (Madam) or, for an unmarried woman, **Cik** (Miss), is the polite form of address to be used with women. If you know the person's first name, this can be added, for example, Puan Rahima, Cik Zaleha.

Pak cik and **Mak cik** (literally "uncle" and "aunty") are slightly less formal ways of addressing someone older than yourself, whom you don't know well. These terms should never be used with social superiors. Although Malaysians will never refer to you by such words, they may disconcertingly use the English "uncle" and "aunty."

Much younger people are sometimes referred to as **adik** (often abbreviated to **dik**), meaning younger sister or brother. This usage is generally confined to Malays.

Saudara/Saudari, literally "relative," is a formal but neutral word that can be used to address adults your own age or slightly younger. **Saudara** is male, **saudari** is female.

Anda is a term coined relatively recently as a neutral form of address in Malaysia and Indonesia. Although used in print as well as TV and radio commercials, you will rarely hear it spoken. It is, however, perfectly correct to use in a formal situation and when meeting someone for the first time.

Kamu, *engkau* (or the abbreviated *kau*), and *awak* (used mostly in Johor) are all familiar forms of "you," similar to "tu" in French and "du" in German. They are used in informal situations with close friends, children or social inferiors, but should not be used generally as a substitute for the English "you."

Tuan (Sir) and *Mem* (Mistress) are words that were commonly used to refer to Western men and women during the colonial era. Malaysians (especially by service staff in hotels, transport workers and so on) may address you by these terms as a matter of courtesy, but you should never use them yourself to refer to Malaysians.

Note: Various terms not in Bahasa Malaysia, but from different dialects and languages, are frequently used by Malaysians of all ethnic backgrounds to refer to Chinese and Indian Malaysians. These generally mean "brother," "sister," "uncle," "aunty," "grandmother" and "grandfather."

Malaysia is a multi-cultural nation comprising Malays, Chinese, Indians and other ethnic groups.

Summary

The following is a brief dialogue between a foreigner (F) and a Malaysian (M) who works in a hotel.

M: *Selamat pagi, tuan!*   Good morning, sir.

F: *Selamat pagi!*   Good morning!

M: *Tuan mau/nak ke mana?*   Where are you going, sir?

F: *Saya mau/nak ke restoran.*   I am going to the restaurant.

Pronouns

Because of the importance of politeness in Malaysian society and the sense of social hierarchy involved in the use of personal pronouns, Malaysians prefer to use first names or the polite forms of address given on pages 16–17 rather than these personal pronouns. When speaking with someone you are meeting for the first time or meeting on a more formal basis, it is more polite to refer to them as *Encik*, *Puan* or *Cik* rather than using the pronouns for "you."

	singular	plural
1st person	I *saya, aku*	we *kita, kami*
2nd person	you *anda, saudara, kamu, engkau*	same as singular
3rd person	he, she, it *dia*	they *mereka*

Note: Malaysian pronouns do not distinguish gender. Thus *dia* may mean "he," "she" or "it."

1st person (singular): I *saya, aku*

Use your own name with people who know you, or else the pronoun *saya*, which generally means "I." *Aku* also means "I" but is used in more informal circumstances, among friends. Note that when requesting something, words for "I" are often omitted because this is understood.

1st person (plural): we *kita, kami*

Kami means "we" or "us" but formally excludes the person or persons being addressed, whereas *kita* includes the person or persons to whom you are speaking. In everyday speech, *kita* is, in fact, used in both contexts and you may generally use this form to translate the English "we."

2nd person (singular): you
anda, saudara, kamu, engkau, Encik, Puan, Cik

Use **Encik** or **Puan/Cik**. In informal circumstances, the first name alone may also be used. If the person being addressed is about the same age as yourself, use **anda** or **saudara**. **Kamu** or **engkau** may be used for children or if you know the person well.

Malaysians often avoid the tricky question of choosing the right word for "you" by using the person's first name rather than the second person singular. Thus, they might ask someone called Zarina "Where is Zarina (or Cik/Puan Zarina) going?" rather than a direct "Where are you going?" You may find it easier to do the same, once you know a person's name.

2nd person (plural): you all
anda, saudara, kamu, engkau, encik, puan, cik

3rd person (singular): he, she, it
dia

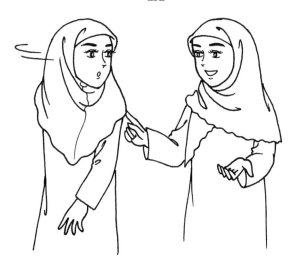

Zarina nak pergi ke mana?

For animate objects and persons, use *dia*. For inanimate things, use *ini* (this one) or *itu* (that one), to mean "it."

3rd person (plural): they

mereka

Basic Vocabulary

The following are essential words for basic "survival" Bahasa Malaysia. We suggest that you make a set of flashcards to help you learn them quickly.

tidak no, not	*ya, ia* yes
ada to have, there is	*mau/nak* to want, wish
boleh to be able, can	*tengok* to look at
datang to arrive	*dari* from
pergi to go, to leave	*ke* to, toward
jalan to walk, travel, street	*di* in, at
sini here	*sana* there
dalam in	*luar* out
makan to eat	*minum* to drink
beli to buy	*jual* to sell
harga price	*bayar* to pay
mahal expensive	*murah* cheap
lagi again, more	*wang/duit* money
cukup enough	*sekarang* now
terlalu too, very	*semua* all
banyak much, many	*sedikit* few, little
lebih greater, more	*kurang* fewer, less
habis gone, finished	*masih ada* still, remain
jauh far	*dekat* near
hari day	*malam* night
pagi morning	*tengah hari* midday

bilik room

bagus good

besar big

sudah already

kereta car

buruk bad, ugly

kecil small

belum not yet

Questions

As in English, interrogative words and phrases are used to form questions.

Apa?	What?
Apa ini?	What is this?
Siapakah?	Who?
Kalau?	If? What about?
Bukankah?	Isn't it?
Kenapa?	Why?
Mana?	Where?
Bagaimana?	How?
Yang mana?	Which one?
Di mana?	Where is it?
Ke mana?	Where to?

Mau ke mana?

Dari mana?   Where from?

Bila?   When?

Note: The word *bukan* (not) is often added at the end of a statement to make it a question, in much the same way as "isn't it" is used in English. *Bukan* is frequently abbreviated to *kan*.

Kan kereta Encik Ramli hitam? or

Kereta Encik Ramli hitam, kan?
Encik Ramli's car is black, isn't it?

Their frequent usage of this expression leads Malaysians to sometimes use "isn't it" incorrectly when speaking English (e.g. "We are going to meet at eight this evening, isn't it?").

Bila datang di sini? When did you arrive here?
(lit: When-arrive-at-here?)

Tuan/Puan dari mana? Where are you from?
(lit: Sir/Madam-from-where?)

Siapa nama Tuan/Puan? What is your (his, her) name?
(lit: Who-name-Mr/Mrs?)

Bagaimana saya boleh...? How can I...?
(lit: How-I-can-...?)

Kenapa tidak boleh...? Why can't I...?
(lit: Why-not-can-...?)

Nak/Mau ke mana? Where are you going?
(lit: Want-to-where?)

Kalau ini bagaimana? What about this one?
(lit: If-this-how?)

Di mana...? Where is...?
(lit: At-where-...?)

Di mana tandas/bilik air? Where is the toilet/restroom?
(lit: At-where-lavatory/water room?)

tandas lelaki or *laki-laki*   = men's

tandas perempuan/wanita   = women's

The above question words do not always have to be used in order to ask a question. The fact that you are posing a question can also be clear from the context or by using a rising intonation at the end of the sentence. To be even more clear, you may also introduce the question with **apakah**, which roughly translates as "Is it the case that...?"

> **Apakah masih ada...?** Do you still have any...?
> (lit: Whether-still-have...?)
>
> **Apakah di sini ada...?** Do you have any...here?
> (lit: Whether-at here-have...?)

Simple Phrases

The following are simple sentences that will be used often, and should be memorized.

> **Ada...?** Is there any...? Do you have any? Are there any...?
> (lit: Have...?)
>
> **Saya nak/mau...** I would like... I intend to...
> (lit: I-want...)
>
> **Tidak mau/Tak nak...** I don't want to! I don't want any!
>
> **Saya mau/nak pergi ke...** I want to go to...
> (lit: I-want-go-to-...)
>
> **Saya mau/nak minum...** I would like to drink some...
> (lit: I-want-drink-...)
>
> **Saya mau/nak makan...** I would like to eat some...
> (lit: I-want-eat-...)
>
> **Saya mau/nak beli ini/itu...** I want to buy this/that...
> (lit: I-want-buy-this/that.)
>
> **Berapa harganya?** How much does it cost?
> (lit: How much-its price?) What is the price?
>
> **Saya mau/nak bayar.** I want to pay.
> (lit: I-want-pay.)
>
> **Terlalu/Sangat mahal!** Too expensive!
>
> **Tidak/Tak boleh!** This/That is not possible!

When you interrupt or pass by someone, you can say:

Maaf! sorry or the widely used, "Excuse (me!)."

When an actual apology is required, use:

Maaf! or **Sorry!** I'm sorry!

Maaf, saya tidak/tak mengerti/faham. I'm sorry, I
(lit: Sorry, I-not-understand.) don't (or didn't) under- stand.

Tuan mau/nak makan sekarang? Do you want to
(lit: Mr-want-eat-now?) eat now, Mr?

Puan mau/nak pergi sekarang? Do you want to
(lit: Madam-want-go-now?) go now, Madam?

Requests

Requests may be made in a number of different ways. Note that the English word "please" has no direct equivalent in Bahasa Malaysia, and is translated differently depending on the circumstances and the type of request that is being made. These various translations of "please" should not be confused.

Tolong literally means "to help." It is used to politely introduce a request when you are asking someone to do something for you.

Tolong panggil teksi. Please (help me) summon a taxi.
(lit: Help-call-taxi.)

Boleh means "be able to" or "to permit" and is used in the sense of "May I please…" when asking politely to see or do something, for example in a shop.

Boleh saya tengok ini? May I please see this?
(lit: May-I-see-this?)

Boleh saya cakap dengan…? May I please speak with…?
(lit: May-I-speak-with…?)

Minta means "to request" and is a polite way of asking for things like food or drink in a restaurant. Note that the use of *saya* (meaning "I") beforehand is optional.

> *Minta air minuman.* [I] want some drinking water.
> (lit: Ask-water-to drink.)

> *Saya minta nasi goreng.* I want fried rice.
> (lit: I-ask-fried rice.)

Pesan is another way of prefacing a request, and simply means "to order."

> *Saya pesan nasi goreng.* I ordered fried rice.
> (lit: I-order-fried rice.)

Beri means "to give," and is a somewhat more direct and less polite way of ordering something. It is also used after *tolong* to politely request a specific item or specific quantity of something.

> *Beri air minuman.* Give me some drinking water.
> (lit: Give-water-to drink.)

> *Tolong berikan yang itu.* Please give me that one.
> (lit: Help-give-that.)

> *Tolong berikan dua.* Please give me two [of them].
> (lit: Help-give-two.)

Cuba means "to try (on)" and is also used with verbs such as *tengok* ("to see") in the sense of "Please may I see..." when asking to look at something in a shop window or a display case, for example:

> *Cuba tengok itu.* Please let me have a look at that.
> (lit: Try-see-that.)

Sila means "Please go ahead!" or "Help yourself" and is used by a host to invite his or her guests to do something, or as a response to a request for permission to do something. It is, for example, polite to wait for a Malaysian host or hostess to say *Sila* or even *Mari* (come!) before partaking of drinks or snacks that have been placed before you. (Please note that **sila** is never used in the sense of "please" when requesting an item.)

Sila masuk!	Please come in!
Sila duduk!	Please sit down!
Sila minum!	Please drink!
Sila makan!	Please eat!
Boleh saya masuk?	May I come in?
Silakan!	Please do!

Terima kasih is used to say "thank you." It literally means "to receive love;" it is also used to mean "no thank you" when refusing something being offered.

Sama-sama! ("same-same") or **kembali!** ("return") are the normal responses to **terima kasih**, both meaning "You're welcome."

Sila minum!

Numbers

Ordinal Numbers

se- prefix indicating one

puluh ten, multiples of ten   **ribu** thousand

belas teen   **juta** million

ratus hundred   **bilion** billion

kosong zero			
satu one		**sebelas** eleven	
dua two		**dua belas** twelve	
tiga three		**tiga belas** thirteen	
empat four		**empat belas** fourteen	
lima five		**lima belas** fifteen	
enam six		**enam belas** sixteen	
tujuh seven		**tujuh belas** seventeen	
lapan eight		**lapan belas** eighteen	
sembilan nine		**sembilan belas** nineteen	
sepuluh ten			

dua puluh twenty	**dua puluh satu** twenty-one
tiga puluh thirty	**dua puluh dua** twenty-two
empat puluh forty	**dua puluh tiga** twenty-three
lima puluh fifty	**dua puluh empat** twenty-four
enam puluh sixty	**dua puluh lima** twenty-five
tujuh puluh seventy	**dua puluh enam** twenty-six
lapan puluh eighty	**dua puluh tujuh** twenty-seven
sembilan puluh ninety	etc.

seratus	one hundred
dua ratus	two hundred
tiga ratus	three hundred
	etc.
seratus lima belas	one hundred and fifteen
dua ratus sembilan puluh	two hundred and ninety
tujuh ratus tiga puluh enam	seven hundred and thirty-six
seribu	one thousand
dua ribu	two thousand
tiga ribu	three thousand
	etc.
seribu lima ratus	one thousand five hundred
sembilan ribu sebelas	nine thousand and eleven
lapan ratus ribu	eight hundred thousand

Cardinal numbers

Cardinal numbers are formed by attaching the prefix *ke-* to any ordinal number. The word *yang*, meaning "the one which is," may also be added when no noun is mentioned to convey the sense of "the first one" (literally: "the one which is first"), "the second one," and so forth.

(yang) pertama	(the) first
(yang) kedua	(the) second
(yang) ketiga	(the) third
(yang) keempat	(the) fourth
(yang) kelima	(the) fifth
	etc.
(yang) terakhir	(the) last

Fractions

setengah, separuh	one-half
satu per tiga	one-third
satu suku	one-fourth
tiga per empat	three-fourths
dua per lima	two-fifths
dua setengah	two and a half

Money

Note: The Malaysian unit of currency is the Malaysian ringgit or dollar, in the past abbreviated as M$ but now officially written as RM. The ringgit is divided into 100 sen (cents).

Harga ini berapa, Puan?
    What is the price of this, Madam?

Enam puluh ringgit. RM60.

Tiga ratus lima puluh ringgit. RM350.

Dua ringgit tiga puluh sen. RM2.30.

Harga ini berapa, Puan?

Etiquette and Body Language

Living in a multiracial society, Malaysians are generally tolerant of the behaviour of others. However, body language is—as in other parts of Asia—as much a part of effective communication as speech. By it, you may either offend someone or put them at ease.

Appropriate dress is important; casual dress in the wrong situation may well be construed as a lack of respect, although many Malaysians are too polite to voice any opinion. While shorts and t-shirts are acceptable in beach resorts, hotels and in tourist shops, it is considered more polite for men to wear long pants and a shirt (either a polo shirt ocotton shirt with a collar), and for women to dress similarly or in a knee-length dress. Sarongs should not be worn in public by foreigners.

Correct dress is particularly important when you are visiting Malaysian friends and government offices. When visiting mosques, women should wear knee-length dresses with sleeves, although they may still be asked to wear an all-enveloping long shawl by mosque officials.

Avoid using the left hand to give or receive anything. Muslims consider using the left hand unclean and always use their right hand to eat with.

It is considered aggressive to put your hands on your hips or to cross your arms in front of you when you are speaking with someone.

For reasons of cleanliness, footwear is almost always taken off when visiting a Malaysian home. Men may wear their socks, if they happen to have them. Sandals are acceptable for both men and women, except on formal occasions, when men should wear proper shoes.

Except for the more Westernized Malaysians, it is not normal to display affection in public by kissing and hugging.

Malaysians are particular about personal cleanliness, and normally bathe twice a day.

When visiting a Malaysian home, it is normal to greet the head of the household first. It is polite to shake hands gently, to nod your head and say your name while doing so. You will be introduced to all the adults in the house (except in some very conservative homes where the women may stay out of sight), and will need to go through a litany of "small talk" questions and answers.

When you are offered food and drink, wait for **Sila!** or **Silakan!** before starting. Don't finish food or drink completely, as this is a sign that you want more. If you do want more, wait for your host or hostess to offer. If you have been invited to a Malay wedding or other festival, don't be surprised if you are presented with your food at

Silakan masuk.

a table set with a fork and spoon, while others are comfortably arrayed on mats on the floor, eating with their hands. You are being honoured by such treatment, so don't insist on joining everyone else on the mats.

If you are in a **kampung** (village) home, don't be surprised if every child in the vicinity crowds onto the verandah to stare at you. They are only being curious and friendly.

When leaving, say goodbye to all the adults in the house, shaking hands again and telling them why you have to leave.

Puan mau yang mana?

Grammar

Verbs

The verb is the heart of the Bahasa Malaysia sentence. The following is a list of verbs that are commonly used in everyday speech. We suggest you memorize them, since they will occur again and again.

ada to be, have, exist	*cakap* to speak
mau/nak to want (= will)	*perlu* to need
suka to like	*tahu (tau)* to know
dapat to get, reach, attain	*punya* to own
boleh to be able to (= can)/ to be permitted, allowed to (= may)	
harus/mesti to be necessary (= must)	
jadi/berlaku to become, happen	

Common verbs of motion (intransitive)

datang/tiba to come, arrive	*duduk* to sit
ikut to accompany, go along	*jalan* to walk, travel
keluar to go out, exit	*masuk* to go in, enter
pergi to go	*berhenti* to stop
pulang to go back [home]	*pulang* return
mula to begin	*lari* to run, flee
turun to come down, get off (a bus, etc.)	

Common verbs of action (transitive)

ambil to take, get	***bawa*** to carry
beli to buy	***cari*** to look for, seek
dengar to hear	***beri*** to give
tengok, lihat to see	***naik*** to ride, go up, climb up
pakai/guna to use, wear	***sewa*** to rent
taruh/letak to put, place	***terima*** to receive

The verb "to be"

Note that the English verb "to be" is rarely translated in Bahasa Malaysia. Sentences of the sort X is Y in English are translated by simply juxtaposing X with Y. The verb "to be" is then understood.

Saya orang Amerika. I [am] an American.

Hotel itu mahal. That hotel [is] expensive.

Restoran ini bagus. This restaurant [is] good.

Restoran ini bagus.

Adalah may sometimes be used to join two nouns in the sense of X is Y although this is usually optional. (*Adalah* cannot be used in this way, however, to join a noun with an adjective.)

> *Saya* adalah *orang Inggeris.* I *am* British/English.

> *Dia* adalah *orang yang pandai.* He *is* a clever person.

Word order

The standard or basic word order in Malaysian sentences is the same as in English, namely:

> **subject + verb + object + complement.**

> *Saya perlu teksi.* I need a taxi.

> *Saya perlu teksi pagi esok.*
> I need a taxi tomorrow morning.

> *Kita/Kami mencari hotel.* We are looking for a hotel.

> *Saya mau/nak sewa bilik.* I want to rent a room.

> *John datang semalam.* John came yesterday.

> *John tiba semalam.* John arrived yesterday.

> *Dia akan berangkat/bertolak ke Pahang esok.*
> He will leave for Pahang tomorrow.

There is one very basic difference, however. In Bahasa Malaysia, the most important noun or "topic" of the sentence is normally placed first. If the topic of the sentence happens to be the object of the verb, then this will be placed first and the "passive form" of the verb with *di-* will often be used (see below).

> *Tuan mau ke mana?* Where is Sir going?
> (lit: Sir-want-to-where?)

> *Letak buku itu di sana.* Put the book over there.
> (lit: Book-that-put-at-there.)

Buah ini untuk dimakan. This fruit is to be eaten.
(lit: Fruit-this-to be eaten.) (i.e. "Go ahead and eat this fruit!")

Very often the subject of a sentence is omitted as it is clear from the context.

[Awak] mau/nak pergi? Do [*you*] want to go?

[Awak] ada bilik? Do [*you*] have any rooms?

Minta [saya] air minum. [*I*] would like some drinking water.

Boleh [saya] tengok? May [*I*] see?

Verb forms

While verbs are not conjugated for person and number as in most European languages, there are a number of verbal prefixes and suffixes that alter or reinforce the meaning of a verb in various ways. The most common is the "active" prefix **me-**. This and other affixes are commonly omitted in everyday conversation, however. For further information on these verbal affixes, see Appendix A.

Saya mau melihat Taman Negara.
I want to see the National Park.

Saya mau lihat Taman Negara. (same)

The passive form *di-*

The passive form of a transitive verb is formed with the prefix **di-**. Note that the passive form often implies an imperative or a necessity.

Kasut ini boleh dicuba. The shoes may be tried on.
(i.e. "You may try on the shoes.")

Dicuba dulu! Try it/them [on] first!

Nasi ini **di***masak.* This rice is to be cooked.
(i.e. "Cook this rice!")

Tense

Verbs do not change their form to indicate tense. The same form of the verb is used to speak of the past, present and future. Usually it is clear from the context which is intended. To be more specific, auxiliary verbs and words indicating a specific time reference may be added, just as in English.

Saya makan. I eat. I am eating.

Saya **sudah** *makan.* I have *already* eaten.

Saya makan **tadi.** I ate *just now.*

Saya **akan** *makan.* I *will* eat.

Saya makan **nanti.** I will eat *later.*

Present tense

If no auxiliary verb or specific time reference is used, it is generally assumed that one is speaking about the present.

Sekarang/kini ("now") is used to emphasize the fact that one is speaking about the present.

Kita pergi **sekarang/kini.** We are leaving *now.*

Saya mau/nak makan **sekarang.** I want to eat *now.*

Sedang is another auxiliary used in the sense of "to be in the middle of" doing something.

Saya **sedang** *makan.* I am *in the middle of* eating.

Kita **sedang** ber*cakap.* We are *in the middle of* speaking.

Future tense

Akan ("shall," "will") is an auxiliary verb used to express the future.

> *Tahun depan saya* akan *kembali/datang ke Malaysia lagi.*
>
> Next year I *will* return to Malaysia again.

Mahu/Hendak is often used as an auxiliary verb to signify the near future, just as in English. It is then followed by the main verb. In this case, it often has the sense of "to intend to" or "will" do something.

> *Esok saya* mau/nak *pergi ke Gunung Mulu.*
>
> Tomorrow I *want to*/intend to/will go to Gunung Mulu.

Nanti ("later") is also used as a specific time reference indicating future tense, often after *mau* + **verb**.

> *Saya pergi* nanti. I will go *later*.

> *Saya mau pergi* nanti. I intend to go *later*.

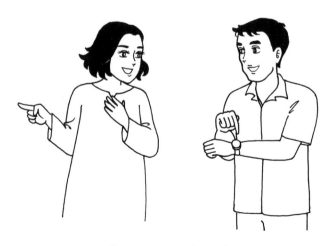

Saya mau pergi nanti.

Past tense

Sudah ("already") is used in Bahasa Malaysia to indicate most forms of the past tense in English. It is placed before the verb, and is often not translated in English. **Sudah** is often abbreviated to *dah*.

Dia dah[sudah] *pergi?* Has he gone *already?*

Ya, dia dah[sudah] *pergi.* Yes, he has gone *already.*

Dah[sudah] *satu bulan saya belajar Bahasa Malaysia.*
I have [already] been studying Bahasa Malaysia for one month.

Semalam ("yesterday") and *tadi* ("just now," "earlier") are specific time references used to indicate the past.

Semalam *saya cakap dengan dia.* or
***Saya bercakap dengan dia* semalam.**
I spoke with him/her *yesterday.*

***Saya datang/tiba* tadi.** I arrived *just now.*

Past tense with *waktu* ("the time when")

Waktu ("time" or "the time when") is another time reference used to indicate actions which occurred in the past. Followed by *itu* ("that"), it means "by that time" or "at that time," and indicates what in English would be a pluperfect tense.

Waktu *dia datang, kita sedang makan.*
When (at the time) he arrived, we were eating.

Waktu itu *saya baru pulang.*
At that time, I had just come home.

Waktu may also be combined with **sudah** to indicate the pluperfect tense.

Waktu *dia datang, kita* sudah *makan.*
When he arrived, we had *already* eaten.

Waktu itu *saya* sudah *pergi.*
By that time I had already gone.

Past tense with *pernah* ("to have ever")

Pernah is an auxiliary verb meaning "to have been" or "to have ever" done something. When placed before the main verb, like *sudah* it expresses the past tense, but is not usually translated in English. It is commonly used together with *sudah* to emphasize past action.

Saya pernah *lihatnya.* I have seen that.

Saya pernah *melihatnya dulu.* I have seen that before.

Pernah is often used on its own, without another verb.

Anda pernah *ke sana?* Have you *ever* been there *before*?

Saya pernah *ke sana.* I have been there *before*.

When used negatively with *tidak* or *belum*, *pernah* has the sense of "never" or "not yet."

Saya tidak pernah *makan daging.* I have *never* eaten meat.

Saya belum pernah *ke sana.* I have *not yet* been there.

Saya belum pernah ke sana.

Negation

Tidak, meaning "no" or "not," is the most common word used to negate verbs and adjectives.

Hotel ini tidak **bagus.** This hotel is *not* good.

Dia tidak **pergi.** He/She is *not* going.

Kenapa John tidak **datang?** Why *didn't* John arrive?

Whenever possible, however, Malaysians prefer to use **kurang** ("less") or **belum** ("not yet") instead of **tidak** because the latter seems to carry a sense of finality or to be too strong. **Kurang** in this sense may be translated "not really" or "not very."

Hotel ini kurang **baik.** This hotel is *not very* good.

Saya kurang **sukakannya.** I *don't really* like it.

Dia kurang **mengerti/faham.** He *doesn't really* understand.

Kenapa Joe belum **datang?** Why *hasn't* Joe arrived yet?

Belum ("not yet") is also more commonly used than **tidak** as a response to a question involving time or action.

Dia sudah pergi? Belum. Has he gone? *Not yet.*

Anda sudah pernah ke Sarawak? Belum.
Have you ever been to Sarawak? *Not yet.*

Bukan is used to negate nouns rather than **tidak**.

Bukan *ini, itu.* *Not* this (one), that (one).

Itu bukan **lukisan tapi batik.**
That is *not* a painting but a batik.

Itu bukan **masalah saya.** That is *not* my problem.

Jangan! ("Don't!") is used to express negative imperatives instead of *tidak*.

Jangan *pergi!* *Don't* go!

Jangan *laju!* *Don't* speed!

Nouns

anak child	*orang* person, human being
buku book	*nama* name
makanan food	*minuman* drinks
mata eye	*hari* day
kereta car	*bas* bus
bilik room	*rumah* house, home
kerusi chair, seat	*meja* table
tempat place, seat	*bandar* town, city
jalan street, road	*kunci* key
kawan friend	*air* water
suami husband	*isteri* wife
nasi rice (cooked)	*gelas* glass
gunung mountain	*pantai* beach
tiket ticket	*barang* goods, item
hal matter	*masalah* problem
muka face	*belakang* back
bahasa language	*negara* country
sudu spoon	*garpu* fork
pinggan plate	*hotel* hotel

Articles

Unlike English, Bahasa Malaysia does not use any articles
("a," "an," "the") before nouns.

Saya akan naik bas ke Penang.
I will take *the* bus to Penang.

Kami/Kita cari hotel yang murah.
We are looking for *a* cheap hotel.

Kami/Kita mau/nak sewa bilik.
We want to rent *a* room.

Ada kunci? Do you have *the* key?

The sense of the English definite article ("the") can often
be conveyed, however, by the possessive suffix *-nya* (literally: "his," "hers," "its," "yours") or by the demonstra-
tive pronouns *ini* and *itu* ("this" and "that").

*Orang*nya *tinggi.* *The* person [is] tall.

Bas itu *di mana?* Where is *the* [that] bus?

Batik ini *mahal.* *The* [this] batik is expensive.

Batik ini mahal!

Plural forms

Singular or plural forms of nouns are not normally distinguished, and the same form is used for both. Singular or plural are indicated instead by the context, or through the use of other words such as "all," "many," etc.

Semua *orang berpuas hati/gembira.*
All the people were pleased.

Banyak *pelancong tiba/datang.*
Many tourists arrived/came.

Duplicating a noun may emphasize that it is plural.

kanak-kanak children

buku-buku books

However, duplication really carries the meaning "a variety of." It is also used to create new words with very different meanings from the simple forms. It is best therefore to avoid duplication to indicate the plural unless you know what you are saying.

Kanak-kanak.

mata eye   *mata-mata* spy

semata-mata only, exclusively

Para indicates plural for persons.

> **para** *penumpang* passenger*s*
>
> **para** *penonton* audience, viewer*s*

Note: More information concerning noun formation using prefixes and suffixes is given at the back of this book.

Classifier words

A number cannot be placed before many Malaysian nouns without the use of certain "classifier words" between the number and the noun. This is analagous to the use of words in English such as "two *pieces* of cake" or "three *sheets* of paper," etc. Some of the more common classifiers are listed below. Don't be concerned if you have difficulty remembering them, however, as you will probably be understood anyway.

> *batang* (lit: "trunk") used for cigarettes, trees, etc.
>
> *biji* (lit: "seed") used for small objects; fruits
>
> *buah* (lit: "fruit") used for larger and abstract things
>
> *ekor* (lit: "tail") used for animals
>
> *helai* (lit: "sheet") used for paper
>
> *lembar* (lit: "sheet") used for paper, wood, etc.
>
> *orang* (lit: "person") used for people
>
> *pasang* (lit: "pair") used for socks, trousers, etc.
>
> *potong* (lit: "cut") used for bread, cloth, etc.
>
> *lidi* (lit: "stick") used for satay, skewers, etc.
>
> *tiga* **orang** *doktor* three doctors
>
> *dua* **ekor** *ayam* two chickens
>
> *sepuluh* **batang** *rokok* ten cigarettes
>
> *dua* **potong** *roti* two slices of bread
>
> *lima* **pucuk** *surat* three letters

Adjectives

Some common adjectives are listed below, together with their opposites.

baru new	***lama*** old (of things/ of time)
muda young	***tua*** old (of persons)
baik, bagus good	***buruk*** old (clothes, things) bad (behaviour) ugly (looks)
besar big	***kecil*** small
mahal expensive	***murah*** cheap
tinggi tall, high (height)	***pendek*** short
panjang long (length)	***lebar*** wide (width)
perlahan slow	***cepat*** fast
penuh full	***kosong*** empty
sama the same	***lain*** different
ringan light	***berat*** heavy
mudah, senang easy	***susah, sukar*** difficult

Noun modifiers such as adjectives and possessives always follow the word being modified, with the relative pronoun ***yang*** (meaning "[the one] which") sometimes intervening (see below).

kereta baru new car

kereta yang baru the new car
(lit: "the car which is new")

gadis/perempuan (yang) muda (the) young girl

orang (yang) baik (the) good person

bangunan (yang) tinggi (the) high building

buku saya my book

rumah anda your house

anak dia or ***anaknya*** his/their child (-nya = dia)

negara kita our country

Comparatives and superlatives

baik	***lebih baik***	***paling baik***
good	better	best
cepat	***lebih cepat***	***paling cepat***
fast	faster	fastest
tinggi	***lebih tinggi***	***paling tinggi***
tall	taller	tallest

Lebih ("more") and ***kurang*** ("less") are used with adjectives to form comparatives. If the thing being compared to is mentioned, this follows the word ***daripada*** ("than") or ***berbanding*** ("compared to").

Dia lebih ***pintar.***
  He/She is cleverer.

Dia lebih ***pintar*** daripada ***saya.***
  He/She is cleverer than I.

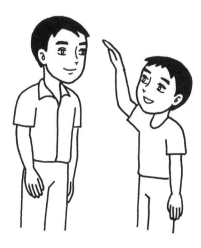

Awak lebih tinggi dari saya.

Rozita lebih *muda* daripada *Peter.*
Rozita is younger than Peter.

Hotel ini lebih *baik* daripada yang *itu.*
This hotel is better than that one.

Dia lebih *tinggi* daripada *saya.*
He/She is taller than I am.

Bas ini lebih *cepat* daripada yang *itu.*
This bus is faster than that one.

Ini kurang *baik.*
This one is not as good.

Ini kurang *baik* dibandingkan dengan *itu.*
This [one] is not as good as that [one].

Amat kurang *tinggi* dibandingkan dengan *John.*
Amat is not as tall as John. (lit: "less tall compared to John")

Note: *Daripada* is used to indicate "from" (with regard to time, source and when making comparisons) and is certainly not shortened to *dari.* *Dari* is used to indicate "from" as in place, for example, **Surat itu dari Johor Bahru.** (The letter is from Johor Bahru).

Batik ini lebih mahal daripada yang *itu.*
This batik is more expensive than that one.

Paling ("the most") is used to form the superlatives "most," "-est." Another way is to add the prefix **ter-**.

paling *baik,* ter*baik* the best

paling *mahal,* ter*mahal* the most expensive

paling *baru,* ter*baru* the newest

Note: The duplicated form **paling-paling** means "at most."

Ke Kota Tinggi paling-paling *perlu dua jam.*
To (get to) Kota Tinggi requires *at most* two hours.

Equality

Equality is expressed by the prefix **se-** ("the same as")
plus an adjective.

> **Dia setinggi saya.** He is *the same* height *as* me.

The construction **-nya sama** after a noun also expresses
equality.

> **Harganya sama.** The prices are *the same.*
>
> **Umurnya sama.** (Our, Their) ages are *the same.*
>
> **Tingginya sama.** (Our, Their) heights are *the same.*
>
> **Warnanya sama.** The colours are *the same.*

Possessives

Like adjectives, possesives follow the noun they modify.

> **Ini buku Eric.** This is Eric*'s* book.
>
> **Ini rumah saya.** This is *my* house.
>
> **Sudah sampai ke hotel Puan.**
>   We have reached *your* (Madam's) hotel.

Punya "to own," "belong to" is a transitive verb that can
be used to emphasize the relation of possession and make
it clearer who is owning what. Note that the principal
topic of the sentence always comes first.

> **Ini saya punya.** This belongs to me.
>
> **Kereta itu siapa punya?** Who owns that car?

The prefix **mem-** may also be added to **punya** to indicate
possession.

> **Hamid mempunyai tiga isteri.** Hamid has three wives.
>
> **Orang itu tidak mempunyai wang.**
>   That person has no money.

The abbreviated forms of personal pronouns **-ku** ("my"
for **aku**) and **-mu** ("your" for **kamu**) may be suffixed to

nouns, but should only be used to address persons one is intimately acquainted with, or children.

Berapa umurmu? What is *your* age?

Itu harapanku. That is *my* hope.

The suffix *-nya*

Adding the suffix *-**nya*** to a noun is equivalent to placing the third person pronouns **dia** or **mereka** immediately after a noun to express possession. It therefore means "his," "her," "its" or "their" (sometimes also "your").

Ini buku John. This is John's book.

Ini buku dia. This is *his* (her, their) book.

Ini bukunya. This is *his* (her, their) book.

This suffix *-**nya*** is also used when a possessive would be unnecessary in English, in which case it takes the sense of the English definite pronoun "the."

Keretanya **di sana.** *The* car is over there.

Hotelnya **di mana?** Where is *the* hotel?

Hotelnya di mana?

Adverbs

Like adjectives, most adverbs follow the words they modify.

> ***begini, begitu*** thus, so   ***juga*** also, too
>
> ***dulu*** before, first   ***saja*** only, just
>
> ***sekali*** very (also "once;" *dua kali* = "twice")

***Dia pergi* juga.** He will go *also.*

***Saya berangkat* dulu.** I am leaving *first.*

***Minta kopi* saja.** I would like coffee *only.*

***Makanan ini sedap* sekali/sangat.**
This food is *very* tasty.

However, the following commonly used adverbs precede the verbs they modify:

> ***belum*** not yet   ***cuma*** merely, only
>
> ***hampir*** almost   ***hanya*** only, merely
>
> ***lebih kurang*** approximately   ***masih*** still
>
> ***sangat*** very, extremely   ***sudah*** already
>
> ***terlalu*** too (excessive)

Saya* masih *makan. I am *still* eating.

Kita* hampir *sampai di Cameron Highlands.
We have *almost* arrived at Cameron Highlands.

Hal ini* sangat *penting.
This matter is *extremely* important.

Saya* hanya *mau/nak beli tiga keping.
I *only* want to buy three pieces.

Barang ini* terlalu *mahal!
This item is *too* expensive!

Prepositions

Di "at," *dari* "from," and *ke* "to" or "toward" are the most common prepositions.

Dia ada di rumah sekarang. He/She is *at* home now.

Saya lari dari sana. I ran *from* there.

Saya mau/nak ke Kuching. I want to go *to* Kuching.

Saya ingin pergi ke Langkawi.
I would like/wish to go *to* Langkawi.

Di is combined with the following words to form a number of common phrases indicating location.

di sini here	**di sana, di situ** there
di dalam inside	**di luar** outside
di bawah below, downstairs	**di atas** above, upstairs
di belakang behind	**di sebelah** next (door) to, beside
di hadapan/depan in front/before	
di seberang across (the street) from	

Imperatives

To form the imperative, the suffix *-lah* is added to the verb.

Pergilah! Go!   **Makanlah!** Eat!

Mari or mari kita are used as hortatives ("come let us").

Mari makan. Come, let's eat.

Mari kita berangkat sekarang. Come, let's go.

Lah is frequently added to the end of a sentence to give emphasis; **Saya terlalu penat, lah!** (I'm far too tired!) Even English sometimes comes in for this treatment, as in the very colloquial "cannot, lah!" (which is best translated as "no way!").

The Relative Pronoun *yang*

Yang is an all-purpose relative pronoun meaning "the one which," "the one who" or "that which." It is most often used in the following construction.

[noun] + yang + *[adjective]*
   the [noun] *which is* [adjective]

If a noun is not specified, it simply means "*the* [adjective] *one.*"

Saya cari batik yang *besar.* I am looking for a large
(lit: "a batik which is large")   batik.

Saya cari hotel yang *murah.* I am looking for a cheap
(lit: "a hotel which is cheap")   hotel.

Yang *hitam?* The black one?

Bukan, yang *merah.* No, the red one.

Yang is also used in certain set phrases like *Yang mana?* ("Which one?"), *yang ini* ("this one") and *yang itu* ("that one"):

Puan mau/nak yang mana?
   Which one would you (Madam) like?

Yang ini? *This one?*

Bukan, yang itu. No, *that one.*

Yang is also used to introduce subordinate clauses, just like the English word "which."

Kain batik yang *kita beli sudah hilang.*
   The batik cloth *which* we bought is missing.

Filem yang *kita lihat itu bagus sekali!*
   That film *which* we saw was very good!

Kawan kawan.

Small Talk

Malaysians are very friendly people, although they are generally too polite to make you feel your sense of privacy is being seriously invaded. They will, if they think you are receptive, strike up a conversation in a bus, on a boat or at a food stall. Common greetings are **Mau ke mana?** or **Dari mana?** "Where are you going to?" or "Where have you come from?" said in much the same way as Westerners say "Hello" or "How are you?." Such greetings do not require a specific answer.

Enquiring about a person's family is considered courteous among Malaysians, so don't be surprised if you are asked if you're married, how many children you have, whether your parents are still alive, and so on. You may sometimes be asked about your religion and even the cost of a certain item you are wearing.

Try not to be offended by such questions, which are just a way of making small talk, in much the same ways as Westerners might discuss the weather or sport. If you don't want to give a direct answer to any questions, just make a joke of it and you won't be pressed.

The following sections will equip you with the basic phrases and vocabulary to deal with the questions you are likely to encounter time and again when travelling in Malaysia, especially in more remote areas.

Name and Nationality

One of the first questions asked, following your name, will be about your nationality.

Nama siapa? or **Siapa nama awak?**
What is your name?

Nama saya Martin.   **Nama saya Jane.**
My name is Martin.   My name is Jane.

Asal dari mana? or **Berasal dari mana?**
Where do you originate from? or Where are you from?

Saya dari Amerika. I am from America.

or **Saya orang/bangsa Amerika.** I am American.

The word **bangsa/orang** (lit: race/people) may be added before the nationality to indicate race or ethnic origin.

(orang) Australia	Australian
(bangsa) Belanda	Dutch
(bangsa) Cina	Chinese
(orang) Denmark	Danish
(orang) Inggeris	British
(bangsa) Itali	Italian
(orang) Jepun	Japanese
(bangsa) Jerman	German
(orang) Kanada	Canadian
(bangsa) Norway	Norwegian
(bangsa) Perancis	French
(orang) New Zealand	New Zealander
(bangsa) Sepanyol	Spanish
(orang) Siam	Thai
(orang) Sweden	Swedish
(orang) Swiss	Swiss
(bangsa) Yunani	Greek

Note that **Inggeris** alone or **negeri Inggeris** means the country England (or Great Britain), **orang Inggeris** is a British person, and **bahasa Inggeris** is the English language. Similarly, **Jerman** or **negeri Jerman** is Germany, **orang Jerman** is a German person, and **bahasa Jerman** is the language. So it is with the other countries, nationalities and languages.

Age

The next thing most people want to know is your age.

> **umur** age
>
> **berumur** to be of the age, have the age…
>
> **tahun** year(s)   **lahir** to be born
>
> **muda** young   **tua** old

Umur anda berapa (tahun)? How old are you?
(lit: "Your age is how many [years]?")

Umur saya empat puluh satu. I am 41.
(lit: "My age is 41.")

Saya berumur tiga puluh tahun. I am 30 years old.

Saya lahir tahun sembilan belas enam puluh satu.
I was born in 1971.

In answering evasively, you may want to joke and say:

Saya sudah tua, mau/nak pencen.
I am already old, ready to retire.

Saya masih muda. I am still young.

Saya masih kecil/budak. I am still a child.

Family

Next you will be asked about your family and marital status. Most Malaysians expect all adults over 25 to be married and all married couples to have children, and will be surprised if they find this is not the case. If you are over 25 and still single, and don't wish to pursue the matter further, you might consider just saying that you are married and have three children anyway (which is what the person asking expects you to say).

bapa/ayah father   *ibu/emak* mother

isteri wife   *suami* husband

perempuan/wanita woman, female

lelaki/laki-laki male, man

kahwin/nikah to be married   *keluarga* family

saudara/saudari male/female

saudara relative

bapa saudara uncle   *emak saudara* aunty

anak saudara niece/nephew

adik (-beradik) younger sibling   *kakak* elder sister

teman wanita/lelaki girlfriend/boyfriend

kawan, teman friend   *orang* person/people

abang elder brother   *anak* child

anak perempuan daughter   *anak lelaki* son

cucu grandchild, grand niece or nephew

ibubapa/orang tua parents

Tuan sudah kahwin ke belum? Are you married yet?

Sudah/Belum. Already./Not yet.

Masih terlalu muda. (I am) still too young.

Tuan ada berapa orang anak?
  How many children do you have?

Saya ada tiga orang anak. I have three children.

Satu lelaki dan dua perempuan.
One son and two daughters.

Tuan punyai adik beradik?
How many brothers and sisters do you have?

Saya punya tiga adik beradik. I have three siblings.

Seorang kakak dan dua orang adik lelaki.
One older sister and two younger brothers.

Additional vocabulary

bayi baby

keluarga relatives, family

datuk grandfather

anak saudara niece or nephew

menantu son/daughter-in-law

bapak/ibu mentua father/mother-in-law

nenek grandmother

pak cik uncle

cerai divorced

ipar in-laws

mak cik aunt

sepupu cousin

Datuk dan nenek.

Occupation

You will then be questioned concerning your job or profession. Many educated Malaysians carry a business card. They may offer you one and ask for yours. After even a brief conversation, many people may ask for your address.

bekerja to work	***pencen*** retired
syarikat company	***belajar*** to study
kad card	***kad nama*** name card

Tuan/Puan bekerja di mana? Where do you work?

Saya bekerja di syarikat... I work at company...

Saya bekerja di pejabat. I work in an office.

Saya belajar di universiti.
I am studying at a university.

Saya menganggur. I am unemployed.

Ada kad nama? Do you have a name card?

Boleh saya minta satu? May I have one?

Maaf, tak ada. I'm sorry, I don't have one.

Additional vocabulary

saintis, pakar sains scientist (m/f)

pegawai white collar worker (officer, clerk)

mahasiswa university student.

ahli sukan sportsman

atlit athlete

wartawan journalist/reporter (m/f)

pensyarah university lecturer

pegawai kerajaan civil servant

pengurus manager *guru/cikgu* teacher

peniaga businessman *pedagang* trader

pekerja kilang factory worker *pelaut* sailor

pengarang/penulis writer *setiausaha* secretary

seniman/seniwati artist

Religion

Although Islam is the official religion of Malaysia, there are large numbers of non-Muslims in the country. All Malays are Muslim, as are some Indians and a few ethnic groups in Sarawak and Sabah. There are many Christians, both Catholic and Protestant, as well as Hindus, Sikhs, Buddhists and Taoists. Religion is considered a politically sensitive subject in Malaysia, and you would be wise to leave it out of your topics for conversation except to answer direct questions about yourself.

agama religion *anggota* member

gereja church *menangut* embrace (a religion)

Tuan/Puan agama apa? What religion are you?

Saya orang Kristian. I am Christian.

Banyak orang Iban begitu. So are many Iban.

Saya orang Islam. I am a Muslim.

Katholik Catholic *Buddha* Buddhist

Kristian, Protestant Protestant *Yahudi* Jewish

Weather

The weather in Malaysia is hot and humid all year round, so there is not much to talk about. One thing that people do often talk about, however, are the rains and great floods or **banjir** that periodically inundate towns along the coasts during the rainy season. People may also ask you how the weather is back home.

There are two seasons, the northeast monsoon (December through February) and the southwest monsoon (May through November). March and April are intermonsoonal periods. The northeast monsoon brings strong winds and frequent downpours to the east coast of Peninsular Malaysia and Sabah and to the southwestern portion of Sarawak, near Kuching. Other areas experience occasional brief showers during this time. When the monsoon changes to the southwest, the west coasts of both the Peninsular and Sabah experience strong winds and regular heavy rain.

banjir flood, flooding	**hujan** rain, to be raining
darjah degrees	**cuaca** weather
matahari sun	**salji** snow
sering often, frequent[ly]	**suhu** temperature
panas hot	**sejuk** cold
cerah clear	**mendung** cloudy
segar fresh, invigorating	**dingin** cool
musim season	**iklim** climate

musim panas hot season

musim luruh fall (*luruh* = "fall")

musim sejuk winter (cold season)

musim bunga spring (*bunga* = flower)

musim kemarau dry season

musim hujan rainy season

Cuacanya panas hari ini. The weather is hot today.

Suhunya tiga puluh darjah. It's 30 degrees (Celsius).

Hujan sudah mula ke belum?
Have the rains begun yet?

Ya, sudah musim hujan sekarang.
Yes, it is [already] the rainy season now.

Tiap hari hujan. It rains every day.

Tahun ini sering banjir.
This year there has been frequent flooding.

Bagaimana cuaca di negeri Tuan/Puan?
How is the weather in your country?

Sangat sejuk sekarang, ada salji.
It is very cold now. There is snow.

Cuacanya panas hari ini.

Time

minit minute	*jam* hour
pukul o'clock	
hari day	*minggu* week
bulan month, moon	*tahun* year
hari ini today	*semalam* yesterday
besok (esok) tomorrow	*lusa* the day after tomorrow
awal early	*terlambat* late
sebelum before	*sesudah* after
sekarang now	*dulu* earlier, first, beforehand
tidak lama lagi soon	*baru, baru tadi* just, just now
nanti later	*sekejap* in a moment
jarang rarely	*kadang-kadang* sometimes
sering often	*dulu* before, earlier

Pukul berapa sekarang?

Bila Tuan/Puan mau/nak berangkat?
When do you want to depart?

Kita/Kami mau/nak pergi/berangkat hari ini.
We want to go today.

Kita/Kami mau/nak berangkat awal
We want to leave early.

Keretapi itu selalu terlambat!
That train is always late!

Semalam terlambat dua jam.
Yesterday it was two hours late.

Tuan sering datang ke Malaysia?
Do you come often to Malaysia?

Jarang. Dulu pernah datang sekali.
Rarely. I have come once before.

Bila Puan sampai di sini? When did you arrive here?

Baru semalam. Only/Just yesterday.

Bila berangkat? When are you leaving?

Sekejap lagi. In a little while.

Telling the time

Pukul berapa sekarang? What time is it now?

Sekarang pukul sepuluh. It is now ten o'clock.

Just as in English, there are several ways of telling the time in Malaysia. One can say "a quarter to nine" or "eight forty-five" or "forty-five minutes past eight."

Pukul dua belas suku. 12.15

Jam suku selepas dua belas. 12.15

Lima belas minit selepas jam dua belas. 12.15

To express minutes after the hour, the words *lewat* or *lebih* meaning "past" may be used, although these are optional.

> *Pukul dua lewat empat puluh lima minit.* 2.45
>
> *Empat puluh lima minit selepas pukul dua.* 2.45
>
> *Dua puluh minit selepas jam lima.* 5.20
>
> *Sepuluh minit lagi pukul empat.* 3.50

The use of *minit* is also optional, as it is easily understood from the context.

> *Pukul empat kurang sepuluh (minit).* 3.50

To express minutes before the hour, the word *kurang* ("less") must be used.

> *Pukul tiga kurang suku.* 2.45

Fractions are used just as in English.

> *Masih ada tiga suku.* There is still three-quarters left.
>
> *Dari Kuala Lumpur ke Bangkok berapa jam?*
> How many hours [does it take] to go from Kuala Lumpur to Bangkok?
>
> *Satu jam.* One hour.
>
> *Berapa jam ke Penang?* How many hours to Penang?
>
> *Tiga setengah jam.* Three and a half hours.

Periods of the day

In English we break the day into **morning**, **noon**, **afternoon**, **evening** and **night**. Malaysians break up the day a bit differently (the following are approximate times).

> *awal pagi* early morning (5 to 7 a.m.)
>
> *pagi* morning (7 to 11 a.m.)

tengah hari midday (11 a.m. to 3 p.m.)

petang late afternoon to dusk (3 to 7 p.m.)

malam night (7 to 10 p.m.)

lewat malam late night (10 to 12 p.m.)

tengah malam midnight to sunrise

siang daytime (between sunrise and sunset)

Note that these periods of the day are used not only in greetings with **selamat** (see Part One: Greetings), but also in place of the English *a.m.* or *p.m.* in telling time.

pukul sembilan pagi 9 a.m.

pukul sembilan malam 9 p.m.

pukul dua siang 2 p.m.

pukul lima petang 5 p.m.

pukul lima pagi 5 a.m.

Days of the week

hari day

(hari) Minggu/Ahad Sunday

(hari) Senen/Isnin Monday

(hari) Selasa Tuesday

(hari) Rabu Wednesday

(hari) Khamis Thursday

(hari) Jumaat Friday

(hari) Sabtu Saturday

Ini hari apa? What day (of the week) is it?

Ini hari Selasa. It is Tuesday.

Dates

tarikh date (of the month)

Januari	January	*Julai*	July
Februari	February	*Ogos*	August
Mac	March	*September*	September
April	April	*Oktober*	October
Mei	May	*November*	November
Jun	June	*Disember*	December

Hari ini berapa haribulan? What is the date today?

Hari ini dua belas haribulan Julai tahun dua ribu satu.
  Today is the twelfth of (the month of) July, the year 2002.

Saya mau/nak pulang/kembali pada sepuluh haribulan.
  I want to go back on the tenth.

Saya mau kembali pada sepuluh haribulan.

Useful words and phrases

lalu, yang lalu past, last

minggu lalu, minggu yang lalu last week

bulan lalu, bulan yang lalu last month

tahun lalu, tahun yang lalu last year

sejak since

Sejak bila? Since when? For how long?

Sejak berapa lama? For how long?

depan in front

minggu depan next week

bulan depan next month

tahun depan next year

tadi a while ago

tadi pagi or *pagi tadi* earlier this morning

tadi malam or *malam tadi* last night

tadi siang or *siang tadi* earlier today

tadi petang or *petang tadi* earlier this afternoon

nanti later

nanti siang later in the day

nanti petang later this afternoon

nanti malam later tonight

Note: When ***malam*** ("night," "eve") preceeds a day of the week, it indicates the night before that day (i.e. the eve of that day). When in doubt, it is best to state the date when fixing an appointment in order to remove any ambiguity.

malam Sabtu Saturday eve (= Friday night)

Sabtu malam Saturday night

Ke Johor Baru lalu mana?

Travel

Asking Directions

alamat address

kampung village

bandar city, town, downtown

stesyen minyak gas station

padang town green

bangunan building

rumah house/home

asrama hostel

tempat place

wisma house (in an institutional sense); public building

lorong alleyway, lane

jalan kecil side street

jalan raya highway

lewat to pass, go by way of

kanan right

terus straight

jalan street

jalan besar main street

jalan tol tollroad

belok to turn

kiri left

lebih-kurang approximately

Malaysians are more than willing to give you directions if they can understand what you are asking them. Note that since the place you are asking about is invariably the main topic of your question, you should always place it at or near the beginning of your sentence (not at the end, as in English). This will make your question more easily understood. It is also more polite to preface any request for directions with the phrase *Maaf, boleh tanya* (lit: Excuse me, may I ask?).

Maaf, boleh bertanya Hotel Majestic di mana?
Excuse me, may I ask where is the Majestic Hotel?

Di mana Jalan Ampang? Where is Jalan Ampang?

Wisma Merdeka di mana? Where is Wisma Merdeka?

Ke Johor Baru lalu mana?
(lit: Which way to Johor Bahru?)
How does one get to Johor Bahru?

Kuantan naik apa dari sini?
How can I get to Kuantan from here?
("*naik*" indicates mode of transport; Lit: *naik* = alight)
(i.e. by what means of transportation?)

Terus saja dari sini, lalu/kemudian belok kanan.
Straight ahead here, then turn right.

Ikut jalan ini terus, sampai lebuhraya.
Follow this road straight until the highway.

Kemudian belok kiri. Then turn left.

Berapa jauh (dari sini)? How far is it from here?

Lebih-kurang lima kilometer. About five kilometres.

Note: When asking directions, phrase your question in such a way that it cannot be answered by a simple yes or no. For example, don't say "Is Jalan Tuaran over there?" *Jalan Tuaran di sana?*. The person being asked may not understand what you are saying and may simply respond yes *ya* or no *bukan* at random. Instead, ask "Where is Jalan Tuaran?" *Jalan Tuaran di mana?*

Taxi directions

The following are indispensible phrases for directing taxi drivers.

Tolong panggilkan teksi! Please call a taxi!

Saya mau/nak ke... I want to go to...

Ke lapangan terbang, Encik. To the airport, Mister.

Mau/Nak lalu mana? By which route?

Yang paling cepat. The fastest one.

Saya mau/nak lalu... I want to go by way of...

Terus! Straight ahead!

Belok kiri/kanan. Turn left/right.

Stop! or ***Berhenti!*** Stop!

Di sini! Here!

Pusing/Pusing balik turn around/make a u-turn

Undur Back up

Perlahan-lahan slowly

Cepat/Laju Faster/Speed up

Awas!Berhati-hati! Caution/Be careful!

Ini arah ke utara? Is this to the north?

        selatan? south?

        timur? east?

        barat? west?

Mau lalu mana?

Public Transport

pergi to go	*balik, kembali* to return
berangkat/bertolak to depart	
datang, tiba to arrive	
batal to cancel	*menunda* to tow
naik to ride, to go by (train, bus, etc.), alight	
pulang to go back [home]	
sampai to reach	
jadual waktu schedule	*pejabat* office
tiket ticket	*tempat duduk* seat
pemandu driver	*tambang* fare
kaunter ticket window	
stesyen (keretapi) train station	
hentian (bas) bus terminal	
jalan route, road	
belum not yet	*langsung* direct, non-stop
masih still, left over	*sudah* already
lambat slow	*cepat* fast

Once again, when asking a question, state the main topic first so that the person being asked knows what it is you are referring to.

Hentian bas di mana? Where is the bus terminal?

Stesyen keretapi di mana?
Where is the train station?

Ke airport berapa kilometer dari sini?
How many kilometres to the airport from here?

Tambangnya berapa? What is the fare?

Ke Pulau Pinang (Penang) boleh naik kereta api tidak? Can I take a train to Penang or not?

Keretapi ke Kuala Lumpur berangkat pukul berapa?
What time does the train to Kuala Lumpur depart?

Pesawat ke Kota Kinabalu tiba pukul berapa?
What time does that plane to Kota Kinabalu arrive?

Ke Alor Star hari ini ada bas lagi tidak?
Is there another bus to Alor Star today or not?

Masih ada tempat duduk? Are there any seats left?

Masih ada. Yes, there are still.

Ma'af, sudah habis. Sorry, sold out (finished) already.

Harga tiketnya berapa?
What is the price of the tickets?

Sekali jalan atau pergi balik?
One-way or round-trip?

Sekali jalan. One way.

Harga tiketnya berapa?

Tambangnya lima ringgit. The fare is RM5.

Naik bas ke Kota Bharu berapa jam?
How many hours by bus to Kota Bharu?

Biasanya lima jam. Usually 5 hours.

Bas ini lambat atau cepat? Is this bus slow or fast?

Ada bas ekspres? Is there an express bus?

Berangkat/Bertolak pukul berapa?
What time does it leave?

Ada pendingin udara atau tidak?
Does it have air-conditioning or not?

Bas ke Melaka itu ikut jalan mana?
What route does that bus to Melaka follow?

Sampai di Ayer Hitam pukul berapa?
What time does it reach Ayer Hitam?

Paling cepat naik apa? What is the fastest way?

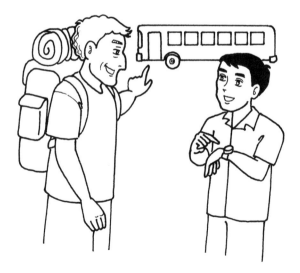

Berangkat pukul berapa?

Letak beg/bagasi di mana?
  Where do I put my baggage?

Sewa kereta ini berapa se hari?
  How much does it cost to rent this car per day?

Dengan pemandu atau tidak?
  Do you want it with driver or not?

Tidak. Saya mau/nak pandu sendiri.
  No. I want to drive myself.

Saya punya/ada lesen antarabangsa.
  I have an international driver's licence.

Modes of transportation

Saya mau naik... I want to go by...

  pesawat (kapalterbang) aeroplane

  kapal ship

  feri ferry

  keretapi train

  kereta car/automobile

  bas (malam) (night) bus

  teksi taxi

  minibas minibus

  ekspres express

  perahu canoe

  sampan small boat

  kuda horse

  beca trishaw

  basikal bicycle

  motorsikal motorcycle

Accommodation

Accommodation in Malaysia ranges from luxury suites costing hundreds of dollars a night to inexpensive dormitory rooms in lodges called ***rumah tumpanggan***. Ask the price of a room first, and have a look at it before checking in. You will have to fill out a registration form and may be asked to pay in advance. Discounts can often be had for the asking.

Check-out time is normally 12 noon. You may be charged for another night if you stay beyond that if you are in an expensive establishment. Most places are very flexible if not too busy. Some Malaysians you meet might invite you to stay in their home, especially in remote areas.

hotel hotel

rumah tumpangan lodge

penginapan small hotel

asrama hostel

bilik room	**kunci** key
beg baggage	**beg pakaian** suitcase
bil bill	**kadar** rate
penuh full	**kosong** empty, vacant

daftar to register

jaminan/wang pendahuluan security deposit

daftar masuk to check in

daftar keluar to check out

cuci to wash	**bersihkan** to clean

Masih ada bilik? Are there still rooms available?

Ya, masih ada. Yes, there still are.

Untuk berapa orang? For how many people?

Untuk tiga orang. For three people.

Maaf, sudah penuh. I'm sorry, we are already full.

Kadarnya berapa? What (how much) is the rate?

Ada bilik yang lebih murah?
  Do you have cheaper rooms?

Boleh saya tengok bilik dulu?
  May I see the room first?

Berapa malam Tuan/Puan tinggal di sini?
  How many nights will you stay, sir/madam?

Tiga malam. Three nights.

Sila daftar dulu. Please register first.

Ini kuncinya. Here is the key.

Tinggalkan kuncinya di pejabat kalau keluar.
  Please leave the key in the office if you go out.

Tinggalkan kuncinya di pejabat kalau keluar.

Saya mau/nak bayar kira bil sekarang.
 I want to pay the bill now.

Tolong ambilkan beg kami.   Please take our luggage.

Tolong berikan kami sikit air minum.
 Please give us some drinking water.

Ada banyak nyamuk.   There are lots of mosquitoes.

Tolong semburkan bilik.   Please spray the room.

Tolong bersihkan bilik sekarang.
 Please clean/make up the room now.

Tolong cuci pakaian ini.   Please wash these clothes.

Note: Boiled water for drinking is normally supplied in a thermos or in a bottle, and you are advised against drinking water from the tap. If you are staying in an expensive hotel, a tip (*hadiah*) of RM1–5 is commonly given to a porter or roomboy, depending on the service rendered.

Tolong ambilkan beg kami.

Useful vocabulary

air con/pendingin udara air-conditioning

kipas angin electric fan

bantal pillow

guling, bantal peluk bolster pillow (Dutch wife)

tuala towel

tilam mattress

kelambu mosquito netting

selimut blanket

kain cadar bedsheet

air panas hot water

gayung water ladle, dipper

bilik mandi bathroom

mandi to bathe

gosok to iron, scrub

tandas toilet

kerusi chair

lampu light

meja table

tempat tidur, katil bed

Note: Bathrooms in cheaper hotels normally have showers but no bathtubs. In remote areas you may find a huge plastic pail of water and a ladle (*gayung*) for scooping water over your body instead of a shower.

Sightseeing

Malaysia's major attractions are scenic. The country has magnificent beaches, islands, rainforests with fascinating plants, animals and birds, plus, in the states of Sabah and Sarawak, caves, impressive mountains, wild rivers and stilt villages over the sea. In Peninsular Malaysia, particularly in Melaka and Penang, there are a number of historic sites and buildings, plus a remarkable and eclectic architecture that blends Chinese, European Georgian, Doric, Corinthian and even a few Malay elements. Traditional lifestyles, particularly on the east coast of Peninsular Malaysia and in Sabah and Sarawak, also attract visitors to coastal *kampung* (villages) and longhouses.

melawat to visit

menonton to watch, observe (a show, film)

pelancong tourist

air terjun waterfall	*hutan simpan* forest reserve
tasik, danau lake	*telaga* pond
pulau island	*gua* cave
gunung mountain	*gunung berapi* volcano
hutan forest, jungle	*mata air panas* hot spring
pantai beach	*rumah panjang* longhouse

kampung air water village (stilt houses over the sea)

pemandangan panorama, view

istana palace	*tokong* Chinese temple
kebun binatang zoo	*kuil* Indian temple
mesjid mosque	*muzium* museum
patung statue	*taman* garden, park

makam, kubur gravesite

menara api tower, lighthouse

pertunjukan performance

tarian dance

wayang kulit shadow puppet show

wayang Cina Chinese outdoor opera

Tuan mau/nak melawat Masjid Negara hari ini?
Do you want to visit the National Mosque today?

Tidak. Saya mau/nak ke istana dulu.
No. I want to go to the palace first.

Mari kita menonton tarian.
Let's watch a dance.

Pukul/Jam berapa ada pertunjukan?
What time is the performance?

Di Pahang ada taman negara.
At Pahang there is a national park.

Ada kebun binatang di sini? Tidak.
Is there a zoo here? No.

Tuan nak melawat kebun binatang hari ini?

Leisure Activities

baca (buku) to read (books)

berjalan, jalan-jalan to walk, go walking

main to play   *berenang* to swim

tidur to sleep   *televisyen* television

badminton badminton

pawagam movie theatre, cinema

kolam renang swimming pool

padang field

gelanggang court

gelanggang tenis tennis court

tenis tennis   *bola sepak* football (soccer)

pantai beach   *pasir* sand

Saya mau/nak berenang di pantai.
I am going swimming at the beach.

Anda/Awak mau/nak ikut tidak?
Would you like to come along?

Tidak, saya mau baca buku ini.
No, I want to read this book.

Ada gelanggang tenis di sini?
Are there tennis courts here?

Buka pukul berapa? What time do they open?

Mari kita ke kolam renang.
Let's go to the swimming pool.

Mari kita menonton di pawagam.
Let's go to the cinema.

Apakah ada pawagam dekat sini?
Is there a cinema near here?

Ada filem apa malam ini?
What film is playing tonight?

Travel Tips

Getting around Malaysia is easy, with frequent scheduled departures of planes, buses and boats. Unlike many parts of Asia, transport leaves on time (well, most of the time!), fares are set, and foreigners are almost never asked to pay more than the normal fare.

Exceptions to this are trishaws or pedicabs, where you must bargain for what you consider a reasonable fare, and some taxis. In most major towns the taxis have meters, but in many areas there is a generally accepted (though not necessarily published) fare. Try to find out from a local what he would pay to be sure you are not asked a special "tourist price."

One useful Malaysian phenomenon is the so-called "out-station taxi," long-distance taxis travelling between towns. These can either be chartered (***sewa khas***) or taken on a shared basis (***tumpang***) with a total of four passengers. Outstation taxis are usually quicker than buses, and as they will go some distance off the main route if you need, even when shared, can be more convenient. They are generally very reasonably priced on a share basis.

Minibuses, holding around a dozen passengers, travel in some areas of Malaysia. They do not follow a fixed schedule but leave when full, and rarely travel after dark. These can also be chartered, but be sure to fix the fare firmly before departure. A minibus or taxi driver will normally be quite happy to return to pick you up a day or so later; they are generally totally reliable, but pay only one way at a time.

Trains, express buses and planes are heavily booked during festive seasons and, to a lesser extent, during school holidays. If travelling at such times, try to book in advance.

Makanan dan minuman.

Food and Drink

Basic Words and Phrases

Dining in Malaysia can be an extraordinarily pleasurable experience, particularly if you are adventurous enough to sample the local cuisine. The following basic words and phrases are designed to help you read menus and order food in Malaysian restaurants.

restoran restaurant

gerai, warong food stall

kedai kopi coffee shop cum casual restaurant

makan to eat	*makanan* food
masak to cook	*masakan* dishes, cuisine
minum to drink	*minuman* a drink, drinks

makan pagi breakfast (lit: "eat morning")

makan tengah hari lunch (lit: "eat midday")

makan malam supper/dinner (lit: "eat night")

sejuk cold	*panas* hot (temperature)
pesan to order	*lagi* more
bil bill	*menu* menu

pisau knife	*garpu* fork
sudu spoon	*pinggan* plate
gelas glass	*mangkuk* bowl
cawan cup	*tisu* paper napkins

Ada masakan Melayu di sini?
　Do you have Malay food here?

Boleh tengok menu makanan?
　May [I, we] see the menu?

Saya mau/nak pesan...　I would like to order...

　satu/satu keping/satu pinggan...
　　one portion of.../a piece of.../a plate of...

　setengah...　half a portion of...

Minta garpu dan sudu.
　Please give me a fork and spoon.

Tolong bawakan garpu dan sudu.
　Bring me a fork and spoon, please.

Minta satu lagi.　I would like one more.

Ada minuman sejuk (dari peti sejuk)?
　Do you have cold drinks (from the refrigerator)?

Berikan satu botol bir sejuk.
　Give me one bottle of cold beer.

Tak mau/nak ais.　I don't want ice.

Minta gelas kosong.　I would like an empty glass.

Minta bil.　I would like the bill.

Note: When eating informally at home, many Malaysians use the fingers of the right hand without any utensils. You will sometimes see people eating this way in street-side stalls, in small restaurants and coffee shops serving Malay or Indian food. When eating out in restaurants, however, forks and spoons are more commonly used. Table knives are found only in Western restaurants serving dishes like steak, while chopsticks are provided in Chinese restaurants, coffee shops and market stalls.

Basic Food Terms

air (pron: "ayer") water

air minum drinking water

keju cheese

tauhu soybean curds, tofu

taukwa hard soyabean curd

tempe soybean cakes

sup soup

biskut biscuit, cookie

mihun rice vermicelli

nasi cooked rice

gula sugar

kuah gravy

roti bread

telur egg

mi wheat noodles

kek cake

kuih traditional cakes

Note: Most meals in Malaysia centre around rice as the staple. Anything without rice is only considered a snack or a light meal. Noodles are a common light lunch or snack and are widely available, especially in coffee shops and Chinese restaurants. *Tauhu* and *tempe* are inexpensive meat substitutes made from soybeans. They are now extremely popular in the West because they are high in protein yet low in fat and cholesterol.

Vegetables *Sayuran*

bawang onion

bayam spinach

pek chye, pak choy Chinese cabbage

jagung corn

kacang beans, nuts

ubi kentang potatoes

kacang kapri snowpeas

selada lettuce

timun cucumber

lobak merah carrot

bawang putih garlic

kacang boncis green beans

cendawan mushrooms, fungus

kacang panjang long beans

kangkong water spinach

kobis cabbage

saderi celery

terong brinjal, aubergine

tanpa daging without meat, vegetarian

Meat *Daging*

ayam chicken

itik duck

kambing mutton

ekor lembu oxtail

satay grilled meat on skewers

babi pork

lembu beef

hati liver

babat tripe

Seafood *Seafood*

sotong cuttlefish, squid

ikan fish

ketam crab

udang shrimp, prawns

udang galah lobster

tiram oyster

Saya mau pesan roti bakar dan telur goreng.

Cooking Terms

bakar grilled, toasted

goreng to fry, fried

rebus boiled

kering dry

kukus steamed

panggang roasted

muda unripe, young

basah wet

masak well-cooked, ripe, well-done

mentah raw, uncooked, rare

bubur porridge (usually rice, with meat, fish or chicken added)

sup soup

soto spicy soup (with chicken or meat)

Breakfast *Makan pagi*

Breakfast is usually not included in the price of a hotel room in Malaysia. For breakfast, many Malaysians eat noodle soups, tossed noodles (*kon loh mi*) or bread (*roti*) with tea or coffee. In restaurants catering for foreigners, eggs and toast are also served, often with fresh fruit and juices.

mentega butter

roti bakar toast (lit: "burned bread")

jem jam

telur goreng fried egg

telur rebus hard-boiled egg

telur rebus setengah masak soft-boiled egg

Common Menu Items

In many coffee shops, stalls selling various local foods
will generally have a small sign up telling you how much
each dish costs. Others, including small restaurants, may
have a menu on the wall. Many Chinese restaurants and
stalls in either markets or coffee shops rather confusingly
offer "Cooked Food." What they mean is food cooked to
order, rather than ready-cooked food.

Many places that prepare food to order do not have a
menu. Customers generally ask what is good and give
suggestions for its preparation. In Chinese restaurants
you will often get fobbed off with those tourist stand-
bys—fried rice and sweet and sour pork. Be persistent
and ask what is good. You can also have a look at the raw
ingredients and point out what you would like, asking for
someone to suggest the best way of cooking it. Alterna-
tively, look at what others are eating and if you like what
you see, request the same.

Some dishes you may find in coffee shops, simple restaurants and food stalls include:

ayam goreng	fried chicken
gado-gado	Indonesian cooked vegetable salad
kari pap	curry puff, a pastry filled with spicy potato and meat
kway teow goreng	fresh rice flour noodles fried with meat and vegetable; also available in soup
laksa	spicy noodle soup, with either coconut milk (*lemak*) or sour fishy gravy (*Penang laksa*)
mee siam	a Malay version of Thai noodles using rice vermicelli; has egg, beancurd and spicy gravy

mi goreng	fried noodles with vegetables, meat and often prawns (also spelled *mee*)
mihun goreng	fried rice vermicelli, similar to fried *mi*
murtabak	similar to *roti*, but with a filling of minced meat or chicken and onion. With peanut sauce
nasi ayam	chicken either steamed or fried, served with rice, cucumber, chilli/ginger paste (*sambal*) and a bowl of chicken broth. The Hainanese Chinese version is universally acknowledged to be the best.
nasi campur	a plate of rice with dollops of vegetable, fish and meat that you select from the range on display
nasi goreng	fried rice with vegetables, egg, usually some meat and prawns
nasi lemak	breakfast favourite of rice cooked in coconut milk with fried fish, egg, cucumber and fried peanut garnish
popiah	fresh spring rolls with savoury filling

Nasi lemak

or luah/or chien   omelette with tiny sweet oysters

rojak   a salad of cucumber, yam bean and pineapple with a pungent dressing

roti canai   flaky pancake served with spicy gravy and lentil stew

satay   skewers of marinated lamb, beef, chicken or pork cooked over charcoal and served with a spicy peanut sauce

sup kambing   Indian mutton soup, rich and spicy, usually served with French bread

soto ayam   Javanese-style soup with chicken, noodles, potato cake or compressed rice cakes in a spicy broth

won ton mi   Chinese noodles tossed with vegetable, usually a little red-cooked pork. Served with broth with pork-stuffed ravioli

Note: If you want to check whether any prepared dishes, especially those in a gravy, are laden with chillies, ask whether they are "hot." (**Pedas atau tidak?** Spicy or not?)

Buah-buahan.

Condiments and Snacks

acar pickles

garam salt

halia ginger

kicap soy sauce

lada hitam black pepper

chilli chilli pepper

keropok udang prawn crackers

keropok ikan fish crackers

kuah kacang peanut sauce

sos cili chilli sauce

sambal chilli paste

sambal belacan chilli sauce with fermented prawn paste

gula-gula candy

gula sugar

madu honey

kacang nuts, beans

sos tomato tomato sauce

Fruit *Buah-buahan*

anggur grape

chiku sapodilla

durian durian

oren orange

apel apple

belimbing starfruit, carambola

limau nipis lime

limau kasturi small sweet lime

limau barli pomelo (fruit like a large grapefruit)

kelapa coconut

nanas pineapple

pisang banana

mangga mango

nangka jackfruit

papaya, buah betik papaya

rambutan small, hairy red fruit, like a lychee

tembikai/semangka watermelon

Note: The variety of fruit in Malaysia is astounding. Some, like durians and mangoes, are seasonal. Many others, like bananas, papayas and pineapples are available all year round. It is fun to poke around in the markets, and also cheaper to buy your fruit here.

Drinks *Minuman*

air botol bottled water

air ais ice water

air limau lime juice (sweetened)

air soya soyabean milk

air minum drinking water

air suam lukewarm drinking water

air masak/suam boiled water

air panas hot water

air bandung cold milk with rose syrup

jus juice   *ais jus* iced juice

wain wine   *minuman keras* beer/liquor

kopi or *kopi susu* coffee (with milk and sugar)

kopi-o sweet black coffee without milk

kopi-o kosong black coffee without milk or sugar

susu milk

susu panas hot sweetened milk

teh ais ice tea

teh panas hot tea with sugar

teh pahit hot tea with no sugar

teh susu tea with sugar and milk

air kelapa muda sejuk iced young coconut drink

Lots of drinks, including most soft drinks, are known by their brand names. These include Coca Cola, 7 Up, Sprite, Fanta, Milo, Ovaltine, and so forth.

Most drinks—including coffee, tea and fruit juices—come heavily sweetened with sugar. If you want them without sugar, or with only a little sugar, you have to specify this when you order (*tanpa gula* = "without sugar;" *kurang manis* = "not too sweet"). Coffee and tea are normally served with sweetened condensed milk. If you don't want milk, add an "o;" ***kopi-o***, ***teh-o***. Finally, you need to specify if you want the drink hot or cold.

>***pahit*** bitter
>
>***teh-o*** sweet black tea without milk
>
>***teh-o kosong*** black tea without sugar
>
>***teh susu panas*** hot tea with milk and sugar
>
>***tanpa gula, kosong*** without sugar
>
>***gula sedikit, kurang manis*** a little sugar only
>
>***ais limau gula sedikit*** iced lime juice with only a little sugar

Taste

masam sour	***masin*** salty
manis sweet	***pahit*** bitter
pedas hot (spicy)	***segar*** fresh
sedap tasty, nice, delicious	
kurang sedap not so tasty	
biasa saja so-so	***rasa*** to feel, taste

Puan suka masakan Malaysia?
Do you like Malaysian cooking?

Ya, sedap sekali. Yes, it is very tasty.

Tidak terlalu pedas untuk Puan?
It's not too hot for you, Madam?

Ya, sedikit pedas tapi sedap. Yes, a bit hot, but tasty.

Masakan di restoran ini kurang sedap.
The food at this restaurant is not so tasty.

Ya, ayam itu terlalu masin.
Yes, the chicken is too salty.

Dan sopnya masam sekali. And the soup is very sour.

Tapi nasi gorengnya sedap!
But the fried rice is delicious!

Food Stalls

Food stalls (***gerai makanan***) are very popular and inexpensive places to enjoy a variety of dishes in Malaysia. Reflecting the country's diverse racial make-up, a collection of food stalls will usually offer a range of cuisines, with Chinese, Malay, Indian and even some Western foods. One exception to this is Muslim food stalls where only ***halal*** foods (those conforming to Muslim dietary requirements) are served. This means no pork whatsoever, so don't expect to find Chinese food here.

Notes on Hygiene

An upset stomach is a sure way to put a damper on a holiday, so it is wise to take precautions. Generally speaking, the standard of cleanliness in Malaysian restaurants, coffee shops and other eating places is acceptable, although you would do well to avoid any food stalls that look substandard.

Gerai makanan.

An upset stomach can be a reaction to too much spicy food, or to eating large amounts of the delicious tropical fruit available in Malaysia. However, it can also be the result of germs picked up from food or utensils that are not hygienically handled. A few tips that may help you avoid any problems:

Avoid any casual eating shop or food stall that looks dirty, just as you would in your own country.

Although officially it is safe to drink water straight from the tap, many Malaysians don't. Always asked for boiled water. Bottles of mineral water are now sold almost everywhere in Malaysia.

It is normally safe to buy cut fruit from vendors at the food stalls or in a coffee shop, but if you have got a particularly sensitive constitution, buy your own in the market, wash them thoroughly and peel them.

It is safe to consume drinks with ice in Malaysia, as ice is made with boiled water.

Malaysians almost invariably wipe their spoons and forks or chopsticks with a paper napkin before beginning a meal, just to be sure they are clean. You would do well to follow their lead.

If you do happen to get sick, the best regime is to eat plain white rice, rice porridge (**bubur**) or unbuttered bread, with plain Chinese tea (without milk or sugar). It's a good idea to travel with an effective anti-diarrhoea medicine; most locals swear by the widely available Chinese "Po Chai Pills."

Boleh saya bantu?

Shopping

Basic Vocabulary

membeli-belah shopping

jual to sell	*beli* to buy
belanja to shop, spend	*rugi* loss
tawar, menawar to bargain	
untung profit	*bayar* to pay
ambil to take	*beri* give

barang goods, item	*harga* price
pasar market	*harga tetap* fixed price
kedai store	*harga biasa* normal price
wang money	*mahal* expensive
wang tunai cash	*murah* cheap, inexpensive

biasa usual, normal	*lelong* cheap sale
rekabentuk design, pattern	
warna colour	*jenis* type, kind
istimewa special	*terbaik* the best

muda young, light (of colours)

tua old, dark (of colours)

sekali very, once

mutu, kualiti quality

terlalu too excessive

Wah! My goodness! (expressions of shock, dismay)

Colours *Warna-warni*

kelabu grey	*biru* blue
coklat brown	*hijau* green
hitam black	*kuning* yellow
merah red	*putih* white

The following is a typical shopping scenario, in which a foreigner (F) enters a shop and is waited on by a shop-keeper (S).

S: *Boleh saya bantu?*
   May I help you?

   Puan/Tuan cari apa?
   What is madam/sir looking for?

F: *Tengok saja.*
   Just looking.

F: *Harga ini berapa?*
   What is the price of this?

S: *Lapan puluh riggit.*
   RM80.

F: *Alamak!/Wah! Mahal sekali!*
   My goodness! Very expensive!

S: *Tidak, Puan. Tidak mahal.*
   No, madam. It's not expensive.

   Tengok kualiti.
   Look at the quality.

F: *Ya, tapi terlalu mahal.*
   Yes, but it is too expensive.

S: *Ya, boleh kurang.*
Yes, [the price] can be reduced.

Puan mau/nak bayar berapa?
How much does madam want to pay?

F: *Tiga puluh ringgit boleh?*
Is RM30 okay?

S: *Tidak, Puan. Saya rugi.*
No, madam. I will lose money.

Lima puluh ringgit saja.
RM50 only.

F: *Alamak! Masih terlalu mahal!*
My goodness! Still too expensive!

Empat puluh, itu sudah harga biasa
RM40, that is the normal price.

Tidak, Puan. Saya rugi.

S: *Ya, boleh.*
Yes, okay.

Puan mau ambil yang mana?
Which one does madam want to take?

F: *Saya mau yang ini (itu).*
I want this one/that one.

Ada warna lain?
Do you have any other colour?

S: *Ada warna merah, kuning dan hijau.*
Yes, I have red, yellow and green.

F: *Berikan dua.*
Give me two.

Satu merah, satu kuning.
One red and one yellow.

Puan mau ambil yang mana?

Bargaining *Tawar-menawar*

By and large, prices are fixed in Malaysia, but there are certain situations where bargaining—which can be great fun—is called for and is acceptable practice.

It is always worth trying to negotiate a better rate in hotels, even large, upmarket establishments, which will often offer a discount if business is slow. You can try asking for a better rate because, for example, it is not a weekend, or you are staying more than one night.

In restaurants, department stores and other large stores, marked prices are not negotiable. However, in smaller shops, especially those selling souvenirs, camera equipment and electronic goods, you should always try to get a discount, especially if paying cash.

You are expected to bargain in markets, when buying tourist items from beach vendors or when taking a trishaw (pedicab). You can bargain from a position of strength if you check the price in advance from a Malaysian. Try asking for a price lower than the first price quoted (maybe as much as 30% less if the amount is large) and then work from there. Use your Bahasa Malaysia, stay calm and collected, and if you think the price is really unacceptable, just smile, say *tidak* (no) and walk away. With luck, the price may then tumble dramatically!

Souvenirs *Cenderamata*

Handicrafts *Kraftangan*

keris ceremonial dagger   *dompet* wallet

kulit leather   *lukisan* painting

payung umbrella   *beg* bag/purse

wayang kulit flat shadow puppets (from animal hide)

wau, layang-layang kite

Woodcarvings *Ukiran kayu*

kayu wood

ukiran carving, statue, sculpture

topeng mask

Textiles *Tekstil*

batik cap hand-printed batik

batik tulis hand-drawn batik

kain cloth (2m)   *sarung* sarong (1.5m)

alas meja table cloth   *selendang* shawl

pua-kumba Iban tie-dyed weavings

Jewellery *Permata/Barangan kemas*

emas gold   *perak* silver

intan uncut diamond   *intan/berlian* diamond

batu permata gems   *batu jed* jade

gelang bracelet   *cincin* ring

anting-anting/subang earring

kalung, rantai necklace, chain

F: *Tolong tanya.* I would like to inquire.

  Kain ini dari mana? Where is this cloth from?

S: *Dari Sarawak, Puan.*
  This is from Sarawak, madam.

F: *Sarawak di mana.*
  Where in Sarawak?

S: *Kain ini dari daerah Rajang.*
  This cloth is from the Rajang region.

F: *Ukiran ini baru atau lama?*
  Is this statue old or new?

S: *Lebih-kurang lima puluh tahun.*
  About 50 years (old).

Clothing *Pakaian*

baju clothes   *blaus* blouse

kemeja, kemeja-T shirt, T-shirt

seluar dalam underpants   *seluar* pants

jaket jacket, windbreaker   *tali leher* tie

kot coat   *cermin* mirror

pakaian dalam underwear   *poket* pockets

sesuai, berpadanan just right, to fit, be the proper size

baju perempuan dress   *tali pinggan* belt

saputangan handkerchief   *selendang/tudung* scarf

kasut shoes

selipar sandals, shower thongs

ukuran measurement

topi hat

S: *Tuan/Awak mau/nak cuba kasut ini?*
   Would you like to try these shoes, sir?

F: *Ya, saya mau/nak cuba yang hitam itu.*
   Yes, I want to try those black ones.

S: *Ukuran Tuan berapa?*
   What is your size?

F: *Ukuran saya tiga puluh sembilan.*
   My size is 39 (European size).

S: *Ini Tuan, cuba dulu.*
> Here they are, please try them on.

F: *Kasut ini terlalu kecil.*
> These shoes are too small.

> *Ada ukuran yang lebih besar?*
> Do you have a larger size?

S: *Ada Tuan. Sekejap.*
> Yes we do, sir. Just a moment.

F: *Ya, ini sesuai.*
> Yes, these fit just right.

Ini Tuan, cuba dulu.

Sundries

Photography *Fotografi*

foto print, photo print *kamera* camera

filem film *lensa* lens

filem berwarna colour film *rosak* spoiled

pecah broken *betul* correct, fixed

membetulkan/membaiki to repair

cuci, mencuci to wash, develop (of film)

Stationery *Alat tulis*

kertas paper *sampul surat* envelope

kertas tulis writing paper *pos kad* postcard

tulis to write *setem* stamps

pen pen

Reading materials *Bahan bacaan*

buku book

kedai buku bookstore

buku panduan pelancong tourist guidebook

kamus dictionary

surat khabar, akhbar newspaper

surat khabar Inggeris English newspaper

majalah magazine

peta map

novel, buku cerita novel

Toiletries

kertas tandas toilet paper	**sabun** soap
berus gigi toothbrush	**sikat** comb
syampu shampoo	**tampon** tampon
ubat gigi toothpaste	**tisu** tissues

F: **Saya mau/nak cuci filem ini.**
I would like to develop this film.

S: **Mau/Nak foto berapa besar?**
What size would you like the prints?

F: **Saya mau/nak yang besar saja.**
I would like large ones.

S: **Macam ini?**
Like this? (pointing)

F: **Ya, betul.** Correct.

Bila siap? When will they be ready?

S: **Satu jam lagi.** In one hour.

Nak berapa besar?

Bagasi ini siapa punya?

Practical Necessities

Telephone *Telefon*

The telephone service works well in Malaysia, and it is even possible to make overseas calls from the Telekoms office in the most remote upriver districts of Sarawak, in the heart of Borneo.

The telephone service was recently partly privatized, leading to the frustrating situation of two different types of card telephones, neither of which will receive the other's card. The use of cards in place of coins is spreading. Cards can be purchased in sundry shops, stationers and from the Telekoms Office.

International Direct Dialling from a public phone booth is easy in Malaysia, and cheaper than using an operator to connect your call. You can either buy a Telekoms phone card which can be used only in the appropriate Telekoms telephones (generally found only outside a Telekoms office), or you can buy the much more widely used Uniphone card. This can be used to call overseas at all Uniphone telephones with an IDD facility. Most telephones outside post offices are Uniphone.

English is spoken by all telephone operators, who are invariably courteous and helpful.

> *telefon* telephone
>
> *nombor telefon* telephone number
>
> *menelefon* to telephone

hubungi to contact, call

sambung to connect

saluran, line line, connection

tekan to press, dial (a phone)

kod code

kod negeri country code

kod daerah area code

sambungan extension

luar negeri overseas

dalam negeri domestic

When you ask to speak to someone, the person answering will normally ask who is calling by saying **Dari mana?** (lit: "From where?") You may either give your name or the place you are calling from.

Halo! Saya ingin telefon ke luar negeri, ke Amerika Syarikat.
Hello! I would like to call overseas to the United States.

Tolong hubungi nombor ini. Please call this number.

Kod daerah lima satu kosong. Area code (510).

Nombornya empat kosong lima tiga kosong lima lima. The number is 405-3055.

Tunggu sekejap. Please wait a moment.

Sedang cakap, tuan. The line is busy, sir.

Sekejap cuba lagi. Try again in a moment.

Silah cakap tuan. Please go ahead and speak, sir.

Wah, tidak ada orang! Oh dear, there is no one there!

Salurannya terputus. The line was cut off.

Boleh saya bercakap dengan Puan Suleiman, sambungan 402?
May I speak to Mrs Suleiman, extension 402?

Dari mana? Who is calling?

Mr Jones. Mr Jones.

Halo, Encik Latiff ada di rumah?
Hello, is Mr Latiff at home?

Telah keluar, Puan. He is out, madam.

Lebih-kurang bila kembali?
Approximately when will he be back?

Cuba/Sila telefon pada jam dua tengahari.
Please call again at two o'clock this afternoon.

Halo. Cik Siti ada? Hello. Is Siti there?

Maaf, salah nombor/sambungan!
Sorry, wrong number/extension!

Encik tahu nombor yang betul tidak?
Do you know his correct number or not?

Halo, Encik Latiff ada di rumah?

Saya tidak tahu. I don't know.

Halo. Cari siapa, tuan?
Hello. Whom do you wish to speak to, sir?

Cari Encik Affandi. I am looking for Mr Affandi.

Dari mana? Who's calling, please?

Kawannya. It's a friend.
(lit: "From a friend.")

Ada. Sekejap saya panggil dia.
He is in. Just a moment, I will call him.

Post Office   *Pejabat Pos*

Post offices are used for a great many purposes in Malaysia apart from sending mail. Make sure you are in the right queue. If you want to buy stamps, look for the counter marked *Setem*; to register a letter, look for the *Pos Berdaftar* counter.

There is no regular position for the collection of Poste Restante (General Delivery) in Malaysian post offices. Enquire at the desk as you enter. Poste Restante should be sent to the General Post Office (GPO) or Pejabat Pos Besar in the appropriate city or town.

Fortunately, there is not a problem with theft of stamps as in some neighbouring countries, but if you are sending very important mail, it is best to register it.

The speed of the mail services varies. For fast delivery within Malaysia or to Singapore and Brunei, use express mail—*Pos Laju*.

Telegrams are sent from a Telekoms Office, always a separate building to the Post Office.

pos post

kaunter counter

bungkusan parcel

surat letter

melalui by means of, via

luar negeri overseas

harga cost

setem stamp

telegram telegram

pakai to use

pos biasa normal (surface) mail

pos berdaftar registered mail

pos udara airmail

pos udara ekspres express airmail

pos laju express airmail (local and international)

Tolong tanya. I would like to inquire.

Di mana saya boleh beli setem?
Where can I buy stamps?

Di kaunter nombor dua atau nombor tiga.
At counters number 2 or 3.

Di mana boleh kirim bungkusan ke luar negeri?
Where can I send a parcel overseas?

Di kaunter tujuh. At counter 7.

Baiklah! Terimah kasih. Very well! Thank you.

Maaf, beratur!
Get in line! (i.e. Don't cut in front of me!)

Puan, saya mau kirim surat ini ke Australia melalui pos udara.
(Excuse me), ma'am. I would like to send this letter to Australia by airmail.

Harganya berapa? What is the cost?

Satu ringgit setengah. One dollar fifty.

Kalau dengan/melalui pos biasa berapa?
How much is it by surface mail?

Lima puluh sen saja, tapi satu bulan baru sampai.
Only fifty cents, but it will take one month.

Baiklah! Saya guna pos udara saja.
Very well! I'll use airmail.

Berikan setem untuk dua surat dan satu poskad.
Give me stamps for two letters and one postcard.

Bank

bank bank   *cawangan* branch

wang money   *wang kertas* notes/bank notes

wang kecil/syiling small change/shilling

duit money   *wang tunai* cash

tukar, menukar to change, exchange

pindahan to transfer

kadar pertukaran exchange rate

Saya mau/nak tukar wang dolar Amerika.
I would like to change American dollars.

Saya mau tukar wang dolar Amerika.

Kadar pertukaran berapa hari ini?
What is the exchange rate today?

Kadar pertukaran tiga ringgit lima puluh.
The rate is RM3.50.

Baiklah. Saya mau/nak tukar seratus dolar.
Very well. I want to change $100.

Customs and Police

bagasi baggage, luggage

beg pakaian suitcase

beg tangan handbag

dompet wallet

curi, mencuri to steal

borang forms

penyeluk saku pickpocket

kastam customs

duti kastam customs duty

lapor report, declare

polis police

balai polis police station

pencuri thief

At customs:

Bagasi ini siapa punya? Whose luggage is this?

Saya punya, Encik. It is mine, sir.

Ada apa dalamnya? What is inside?

Pakaian saja, Encik. Just clothing, sir.

Tidak ada barang untuk dilaporkan.
I have nothing to declare.

At the police station:

Encik, saya kehilangan beg/dompet.
Sir, I have lost my purse/wallet.

Di mana? Where?

Baru tadi, di stesyen keretapi.
Just now, at the train station.

Adakah puan melihat siapa yang ambilnya?
Did you see who took it?

Tidak, encik. Barangkali penyeluk saku.
No sir. Probably a pickpocket.

Baiklah! Ini ada borang.   Very well! Here is a form.

Harus diisi dulu.   You must fill it out first.

Dealing with government bureaucracy in Malaysia can sometimes be frustrating, with certain offices such as Immigration often confusingly crowded. However, staff are usually particularly helpful to foreign visitors, so if you are uncertain about where you should wait or what you should do, don't get upset or angry: just ask for help with an appealing smile. And don't forget, even a few words of Bahasa Malaysia usually works like a charm!

Filling out Forms   *Melengkapkan borang*

The following are common entries on immigration and other forms.

nama name	*alamat kediaman* residence
tarikh date	*umur* age
jantina sex	

surat keterangan   identification papers

pekerjaan   occupation

tempat lahir   place of birth

warganegara   citizenship

bangsa   nationality

tujuan lawatan   purpose of visit

status perkahwinan   marital status

tandatangan   signature

Health and Illness

Sakit is the all-purpose term for "sickness" or "pain," while *ubat* is similarly used to denote any type of medicine. If you are sick, it is easy to consult a doctor and obtain a prescription in Malaysia. Government clinics and the outpatient departments of public hospitals will treat foreigners for a price that is unbelievably cheap, although you will generally need to wait. It is usually better to consult a private doctor. Ask your hotel for a recommendation.

All doctors and most nursing staff speak English, and standards of medical treatment are reassuringly good. There is, however, a tendency in some clinics to issue the dreadful duet (antibiotics and Panadol pain relievers) for just about everything that ails you.

Hospitals, clinics and most medical practitioners (who usually work in a group) maintain their own dispensaries where prescriptions are filled. Pharmacies are well stocked, but you need a doctor's prescription for a number of drugs.

sakit sick

sehat healthy

sakit gigi toothache

sakit kepala headache

sakit tekak sore throat

sakit perut stomach ache, intestinal distress

parah serious (of illness)

doktor doctor

doktor gigi dentist

hospital hospital

kemalangan accident

ambulans ambulance

kecemasan emergency

unit kecemasan emergency room (in a hospital)

makmal laboratory

jururawat nurse

batuk cough

demam fever

cirit-birit diarrhoea

hamil pregnant

lecet scraped, grazed

luka injury, injured

muntah vomit

patah tulang broken bone, to break a bone

selsema, flu cold, flu

pening dizziness, nausea

racun poison

keracunan food poisoning

ubat medicine

farmasi drugstore, pharmacy

antibiotik antibiotics

aspirin aspirin

kain pembalut bandage

preskripsi prescription

suntikan injection

Saya sakit. Ada doktor di sini yang cakap bahasa Inggeris? I am sick. Is there a doctor here (i.e. nearby) who speaks English?

Saya mau ke rumah sakit. I want to go to the hospital.

Tolong panggil ambulans. Please call an ambulance.

Saya mau beli ubat. I want to buy some medicine.

Di mana ada farmasi? Where is a pharmacy?

Ini preskripsinya. Here is the prescription.

Ada ubat untuk batuk? Do you have cough medicine?

Ada ubat untuk selsema?
Do you have medicine for a cold?

Ada ubat untuk sakit perut?
Do you have medicine for stomach ailments?

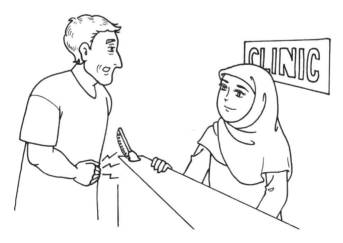

Ada ubat untuk sakit perut?

Parts of the Body

darah blood

otot muscle

urat tendon

kulit skin

tulang bone

kepala head

pipi cheeks

mulut mouth

gigi teeth

mata eyes

rahang jaw

lidah tongue

hidung nose

rambut hair

telinga ear

leher neck

badan body

dada chest, breasts

bahu shoulders

perut stomach, belly

pinggang waist

lengan arm

jari tangan fingers

belakang back

tangan hand, forearm, wrist

kuku nails

kaki leg, foot

jari kaki toes

buku lali ankle

kemaluan genitals

rahim womb, uterus

punggung hips

Verb and Noun Affixes

Bahasa Malaysia has many words that are derived from simple roots through the addition of prefixes and suffixes. For example, the word **baik** alone means "good" and serves as the root for **kebaikan** (with prefix ke- and suffix -an) meaning "goodness." Another example is the verb **tinggal** which by itself means both "to stay" or "to leave." The derived form **meninggal** (with prefix **me-** and substitution of nasal **n** for initial consonant **t-** of the root) means "to die, pass away," whereas the word **meninggalkan** (with added suffix -kan) means "to leave behind."

When dealing with derived forms, there are really two separate problems. First of all, you need to know the mechanical rules for adding prefixes and suffixes to root words so that you are able to do this yourself, and to identify roots of words you come across so you can look them up in a dictionary. Second, you need to understand how the addition of these various prefixes and suffixes changes the meaning of a root.

Verb Affixes

The active prefix *me-* (for transitive verbs)

Most transitive verbs (verbs which can take a direct object) may be prefixed by **me-**. This prefix generally does not change the meaning of the root, but merely emphasizes that a verb is being used in an active (as opposed to a passive) sense, i.e. that the subject of the verb is the main focus or topic of the sentence.

lihat ⇒ *melihat* to see

Saya sudah melihat Muzium Negara.
I have already seen the National Museum.

There are a few idiomatic cases where the addition of **me-** dramatically alters the meaning of the root word, as in the example already given above of **tinggal** ("to stay; to leave") ⇒ **meninggal** ("to die, pass away") where the latter is a shortened form of **meninggal dunia** meaning "to depart the world."

As already mentioned in Part Two: Grammar, the use of such "active verbal prefixes" is often optional, and in colloquial speech the prefix is usually omitted. Note also that this prefix is never used in relative clauses and imperatives.

This active verbal prefix is also used to create transitive verbs out of nouns and adjectives. In this case, the root and the prefixed form have quite different, although related, meanings.

kuning yellow ⇒ *menguning* to turn yellow

kipas a fan ⇒ *mengipas* to fan

kunci a key ⇒ *mengunci* to lock

Rules for prefixing *me-*

The prefix **me-** takes five different forms, depending on the first letter of the word that it is prefixed to. You will need to memorize the following rules for this.

1) **meny-** for words beginning with **s-**

siram ⇒ *menyiram* to sprinkle

surat a letter ⇒ *menyurat* to write a letter

2) **mem-** before words beginning with **b-** and **p-**

   beli ⇒ **membeli** to buy

   pakai ⇒ **memakai** to use

   beri ⇒ **memberi** to give

3) **men-** for words beginning with **d-**, **j-**, **c-** and **t-**

   dorong ⇒ **mendorong** to push

   jual ⇒ **menjual** to sell

   cuci ⇒ **mencuci** to wash

   tutup ⇒ **menutup** to close

4) **meng-** for words beginning with **k**, **g**, **h** or any vowel

   kasih ⇒ **mengasih** to love

   ganggu ⇒ **mengganggu** to disturb

   harap ⇒ **mengharap** to hope

   atur ⇒ **mengatur** to arrange

5) **me-** before all other initial consonants

Note that in the examples given above, the first letters **p**, **t**, **k** and **s** of the root verbs (i.e. voiceless consonants) are dropped when the prefix is added.

The active prefix **ber-** (for intransitive verbs)

The active prefix **ber-** is used with intransitive verbs (those which cannot take a direct object) in much the same way that **me-** is prefixed to transitive verbs. The verb with this prefix has more or less the same meaning as the root, and as with **me-** it is often omitted in everday speech.

   asal ⇒ **berasal** to originate

   cakap ⇒ **bercakap** to speak

   diri ⇒ **berdiri** to stand

   laku ⇒ **berlaku** happen, to carry out

Perkara itu berlaku semalam.
It happened yesterday.

Kami berasal dari Australia.
We are from Australia.

Note that there are a number of irregular forms.

> ***ajar*** to teach ⇒ ***belajar*** to learn

> ***kerja*** ⇒ ***bekerja*** to work

When prefixed to an adjective or noun, ***ber-*** creates an active, intransitive verb that has the meaning "possessing" or "taking the attribute of" that noun or adjective.

> ***kembang*** blossom, flower ⇒
> ***berkembang*** to develop, blossom, expand

> ***bahasa*** language ⇒ ***berbahasa*** to know or speak a language; to be polite

> ***pakaian*** clothing ⇒
> ***berpakaian*** to get dressed, be dressed

> ***kata*** words ⇒ ***berkata*** to speak

Saudara dibersarkan di mana?
Where did you grow up?

Saya tidak berbahasa Malaysia/berbahasa Melayu.
I cannot speak Malay.

Note that before words beginning with ***r***, ***ber-*** becomes ***be-*** (which is to say that only one ***r*** appears in the resulting prefixed form).

> ***renang*** ⇒ ***berenang*** to swim

> ***rancang*** ⇒ ***berancang*** to plan

The passive prefix *di-*

The opposite of the active prefix **me-** is the passive prefix **di-** which indicates that the object of the verb is the main focus or topic of the sentence. This is very similar to the passive voice in English. (See Part Two: Grammar for more examples with **di-**.)

Keretanya belum dibetulkan.
The car has not yet *been repaired.*

Kita diundang *ke rumah kawan.*
We *have been invited* to a friend's house.

Nasinya sudah dimasak.
The rice *has* already *been cooked.*

The perfective prefix *ter-*

The prefix **ter-** is used to indicate that an action has already been completed, with the emphasis being on the resultant state or condition of the direct object. As with **di-**, the focus or main topic of the sentence is always the object of the verb and not the subject. In fact, when **ter-** is used, the subject is often not even mentioned. In this case, the subject is either understood or it may be intentionally left ambiguous as to who or what was responsible for the action.

> *kenal* to know, be acquainted ⇒
> *terkenal* to be famous, well-known
>
> *atur* to arrange ⇒ *teratur* to be well-organized, neat
>
> *pakai* to use ⇒ *terpakai* to have been used

This prefix is often used together with the word **sudah**, meaning "already."

Biliknya sudah *terkunci.*
The room is already locked.

Bil kami sudah *terbayar belum?*
Has our bill been paid yet?

Note: The use of *ter-* as a verbal prefix is distinct from the use of *ter-* with adjectives, in which case it forms a superlative meaning "the most," "the greatest," etc. (See Part Two: Grammar.)

The factive suffix *-kan*

The verbal suffix *-kan* is a factive suffix that creates transitive verbs out of intransitive verbs as well as nouns and adjectives.

selesai to be finished ⇒
selesaikan to finish or settle something

tinggal to stay, to leave ⇒
tinggalkan to leave something behind

kata words ⇒ *katakan* to speak, say

pasar market ⇒ *pasarkan* to market (goods, etc.)

betul correct ⇒ *betulkan* to fix, correct

When *-kan* is added to a verb that is already transitive, it emphasizes that the action is being focused on the direct object of the verb.

Tolong berikan nasi.
Please give [me] some rice.

Suffixed forms with *-kan* may be used in an active sense with *me-* (although the latter is often dropped in everyday speech), or in a passive sense with *di-*.

Saya belum menyelesaikan pekerjaan itu.
I haven't finished that work yet.

Kamera ini boleh dibetulkan tidak?
Can this camera be fixed or not?

The dative suffix *-i*

The dative suffix *-i* is added to intransitive verbs and adjectives to create transitive verbs which imply that something is being done to, toward, for the benefit of, or by the subject. It often conveys a strong sense of location or direction.

> *datang* to come ⇒
> *datangi* to pay a visit to someone
>
> *dekat* close, nearby ⇒ *dekati* to approach
>
> *hubung* connect ⇒
> *hubungi* to contact, get in touch with

Resulting verbs with *-i* can be used both in an active sense with *me-*, and in a passive sense with *di-*.

Saya akan cuba menghubungi anda di pejabat.
I will try to contact you at the office.

The causative prefix *per-* (with *-i* and *-kan*)

The prefix *per-* is a causative prefix added to adjectives to form transitive verbs.

> *kecil* small ⇒ *perkecil* to reduce, make smaller
>
> *besar* large ⇒ *perbesar* to enlarge
>
> *panjang* long ⇒ *perpanjang* to extend

It is most often used together with the suffixes *-i* and *-kan* to produce transitive verbs that indicate that the subject of the sentence is instrumental in bringing about the action or state intended. The form ***memper-*** is used in the active sense, while ***diper-*** is used in the passive sense.

The suffix *-i* is most often used with adjectives and intransitive verb roots, while *-kan* is used with transitive verb roots (but also with some adjectives). The usages of *-i* and *-kan* in these constructions are quite irregular and actually vary with different dialects of Malay.

> ***lihat*** to see ⇒
> ***perlihatkan*** to show (something to someone)

> ***ingat*** to remember ⇒
> ***peringati*** to remind (someone of something)

> ***kenal*** to know, be acquainted ⇒
> ***perkenalkan*** to introduce (to someone)

> ***timbang*** to weigh ⇒ ***pertimbangkan*** to consider

> ***baik*** good, well ⇒ ***perbaiki*** to improve, fix, repair

Important note

The usages of *-kan*, *-i*, *per-* and *ber-* are actually quite lexicalized, which is to say that the resulting forms with these affixes are fairly irregular and idiomatic. You cannot expect to add these affixes to every verb, noun or adjective in the language and get something that makes sense. Rather than trying to figure out the rules under which one form should be used instead of another, you are better off simply learning the resulting verbs with the affixes as separate vocabulary items.

These four verb affixes are therefore quite different from the active, passive and perfective prefixes ***me-***, ***di-*** and ***ter***, which may be used quite freely with any verbs (as well as with many nouns and adjectives).

Noun Affixes

There are a number of different ways of producing nouns out of verbs and adjectives, and even from other nouns. These forms are highly idiomatic, and as with many of the verb forms, you will simply have to learn the nouns derived in this way as separate vocabulary items.

The instrumental prefix *pe-*

The instrumental prefix *pe-* is added to nouns or verbs to produce nouns meaning "one who does" something.

> *laut* sea ⇒ *pelaut* sailor
>
> *main* to play ⇒ *pemain* player

Rules for prefixing *pe-*

As with *me-*, the prefix *pe-* takes five different forms depending on the initial letter of the verb or noun it is attached to.

1) *peny-* before words beginning with *s-*

> *sakit* sick, ill ⇒ *penyakit* illness

2) *pem-* before words beginning with *b-* and *p-*

> *beli* to buy ⇒ *pembeli* buyer
>
> *pakai* to use ⇒ *pemakai* user

3) *pen-* for words beginning with *d-*, *j-*, *c-* and *t-*

> *dengar* to hear ⇒ *pendengar* listener
>
> *jual* to sell ⇒ *penjual* seller
>
> *curi* to steal ⇒ *pencuri* thief
>
> *tulis* to write ⇒ *penulis* writer

4) **peng-** for words beginning with **k**, **g** or any vowel

  karang to write ⇒ **pengarang** author

  ganti to exchange ⇒ **pengganti** replacement

  urus to arrange ⇒ **pengurus** person in charge

5) **pe-** before all other initial consonants

Note that in the examples given above, the first letters **p**, **t**, **k** and **s** of the root verbs (i.e. voiceless consonants) are dropped when the prefix is added.

The suffix -an

The suffix **-an** is added to verbs to produce nouns.

  makan to eat ⇒ **makanan** food

  minum to drink ⇒ **minuman** a drink

  pinjam to borrow ⇒ **pinjaman** borrowings

  tegur to warn ⇒ **teguran** warning

  kenal to know, be acquainted ⇒
    kenalan acquaintance

When added to a noun, the suffix **-an** denotes a noun category.

  sayur vegetable ⇒ **sayuran** vegetables (as a group, distinct from meats, etc.)

The circumfix pe- + -an

The nominalizing circumfix **pe- + -an** also changes verbs to nouns. There is no essential difference between this and the simple suffix **-an** and their usages are simply idiomatic. In some cases, there are even two nouns, one with and one without **pe-**, having the same meaning.

periksa to inspect ⇒ *pemeriksaan* inspection

terima to receive ⇒ *penerimaan* receipts

harap to hope ⇒
harapan, *pengharapan* hope, expectation

labuh to drop anchor ⇒ *pelabuhan* harbour, port

Rules for adding *pe-* here are the same as those given above.

The circumfix *per-* + *-an*

The circumfix *per-* + *-an* is used to produce nouns from certain verbs in place of *pe-* + *-an*. The main difference seems to be that this form has the sense of agency or causation (cf. the causative verb prefix *per-* above), but again, the usages are quite idiomatic and the resulting nouns simply need to be learned individually.

cuba to try ⇒ *percubaan* test, attempt

kahwin to marry ⇒ *perkahwinan* wedding

kembang flower, blossom ⇒
perkembangan development

The circumfix *ke-* + *-an*

The circumfix *ke-* + *-an* is added to verbs and adjectives to produce abstract nouns.

ada to be, have, exist ⇒ *keadaan* state, condition

aman secure, safe ⇒ *keamanan* security

nyata clear, evident ⇒ *kenyataan* facts, evidence

baik good, well ⇒ *kebaikan* goodness

besar large ⇒ *kebesaran* size, largeness

Suggestions for Further Study

The most authoritative dictionary, *Kamus Dewan*, is published in Kuala Lumpur by the Dewan Bahasa dan Pustaka (the Language and Literary Agency).

A number of other dictionaries are available. A practical, two-in-one dictionary—*Kamus Dwibahasa Oxford Fajar, Inggeris–Melayu, Melayu–Inggeris*—is published by Oxford University Press.

The most complete dictionary, listing over 55,000 words of Bahasa Malaysia with examples of how each word is used in sentences, and with English translations, is *Kamus Lengkap*, by Drs Awang Sudjai Hairul and Yusoff Khan, published by Pustaka Zaman Sdn Bhd.

English–Bahasa Malaysia Dictionary

For the sake of clarity, only the most common Malaysian equivalents for each English word have been given below.

In the case of verbs, simple roots are given first, followed by common affixed form(s) with the same meaning, if any. For more on affixation of verbal roots, see Appendix A.

A

able to *boleh*

about (approximately) *lebih-kurang, sekitar*

about (regarding) *tentang, mengenai*

above, upstairs *di atas*

accident *kemalangan*

accidentally, by chance *kebetulan*

accommodation *penginapan*

accompany, to *ikut*

according to *menurut*

acquainted, to be *kenal, mengenal*

across from *seberang*

act, to *tindak, bertindak*

action *tindakan*

active *giat*

activity *kegiatan*

add to *tambah, menambah*

address *alamat*

admit, confess *aku, mengaku*

advance money, deposit *wang muka, cagaran*

advance, go forward *maju*

aeroplane, airplane *pesawat, kapal terbang*

afraid *takut*

after *sesudah, setelah*

afternoon (3 pm to dusk) *petang*

afternoon (midday) *tengah hari, siang*

afterwards, then *kemudian*

again *lagi*

age *umur*

agree to do something, to *janji, telah setuju*

agree, to *setujui, menyetujui*

agreed! *setuju! jadi!*

agreement *perjanjian, persetujuan*

air *udara*

alive *hidup*

all *semua, seluruh, segala*

alley, lane *lorong*

allow, permit *biarkan, perbolehkan, izin*

allowed to (= may) *boleh, izinkan*

almost *hampir*

alone *sendiri, sendirian*

already *sudah*

also *juga*

ambassador *duta besar*

among *antara, di antara*

amount *jumlah, sejumlah*

ancient *kuno*

and *dan*

angle *segi*

angry *marah*

animal *binatang, haiwan*

annoyed *jengkel*

answer the phone *jawab telefon*

answer, response (spoken) *jawaban, jawapan*

answer, to respond (a letter) *balas, membalas*

answer, to respond (spoken) *jawab, menjawab*

ape *kera, monyet*

appear, to *muncul, memuncul; timbul, menimbul*

appearance, looks *rupa, penampilan*

apple *epal*

approach, to (in space) *mendekati*

approach, to (in time) *menjelang*

approximately *lebih-kurang, sekitar*

April *April*

area *daerah, wilayah*

arena *gelanggang*

arm *lengan*

army *tentera*

around (approximately) *lebih-kurang, sekitar*

around (nearby) *dekat, hampir*

around (surrounding) *sekeliling, di sekitar*

arrange, to *atur, mengatur; urus, mengurus*

arrangements, planning *perancangan*

arrival *ketibaan, kedatangan*

arrive, to *tiba, datang*

art *seni*

artist *seniman, artis*

ashamed, embarrassed *malu*

ask about, to *tanyakan, menanyakan*

ask for, request *minta, meminta*

ask, to *tanya, menanya*

assemble, gather *kumpul, berkumpul*

assemble, put together *pasang, memasang*

assist, to *bantu, membantu*

assistance *bantuan*

astonished *hairan*

at *di*

atmosphere, ambience *suasana*

attain, reach *capai, mencapai; sampai, menyampai*

attend, to *hadir, kendali*

attitude *sikap*

auction, to *lelong, melelong*

auctioned off *dilelong*

August *Ogos*

aunt *mak cik, mak saudara*

authority, person in charge *orang yang bertanggung jawab*

authority, power *kekuasaan*

automobile, car *kereta*

available *ada, sedia, tersedia*

available, to make *sediakan, menyediakan, mengadakan*

average (numbers) *purata*

average (so-so, just okay) *macam biasa, sedang, sederhana*

awake, to *bangun, membangun*

awaken, to *membangunkan*

aware *sedar*

awareness *kesadaran*

B

baby *bayi*

back *belakang*

back of *di belakang*

back up, to *mundur, bantu*

backwards, reversed *kebelakang*

bad *buruk, tidak baik*

bad luck *celaka, malang*

bag *beg*

baggage *beg, bagasi*

ball *bola*

banana *pisang*

bargain, to *tawar, menawar*

base, foundation *asas, dasar*

based on *berdasar*

basic *yang dasar, asas*

basis *dasar*

basket *bakul, keranjang*

bath *mandi*

bathe, to take a bath *mandi*

bathroom *bilik mandi, tandas*

bay *teluk*

be, exist, have *ada*

beach *pantai*

bean *kacang*

beat (to defeat) *kalahkan, mengalahkan*

beat (to strike) *pukul*

beautiful (of people) *cantik*

beautiful (of places) *indah*

beautiful (of things) *bagus*

because *kerana, sebab*

become, to *jadi, menjadi*

bed *katil, tempat tidur*

bedroom *bilik tidur*

bedsheet *kain cadar*

beef *daging lembu*

before (in front of) *di depan, di muka*

before (in time) *sebelum*

beforehand, earlier *dulu*

begin, to *mulai, memulakan*

beginning *permulaan*

beginning, in the *pada permulaan*

behind *di belakang*

belief, faith *kepercayaan*

believe, to *percaya, yakin*

below, downstairs *di bawah*

belt *tali pinggang*

best *paling baik, paling bagus*

better *lebih baik, lebih bagus*

between *antara*

bicycle *basikal*

big (area) *luas*

big (size) *besar*

bill *kira, bil*

billion *bilion*

bird *burung*

birth, to give *melahirkan*

birthday *hari jadi*

bitter *pahit*

black *hitam*

blanket *selimut*

blood *darah*

blossom *kembang*

blouse *baju*

blue *biru*

boat *perahu, sampan*

body *badan, tubuh*

boil, to *merebus*

boiled *rebus*

bone *tulang*

book *buku*

border, edge *batas, pinggir*

bored *bosan*

boring *membosankan*

born *lahir*

borrow, to *pinjam, meminjam*

botanic garden *kebun bunga, taman bunga*

both *dua-duanya, keduanya*

bother, disturb *ganggu, mengganggu*

bother, disturbance *gangguan*

boundary, border *batas*

bowl *mangkuk*

box (cardboard) *kotak*

box *kotak, peti*

boy *anak laki-laki*

bracelet *gelang*

branch *cabang*

brand *cap*

brave, daring *berani*

bread *roti*

break apart, to *pisah, terpisah, patah*

break down, to (of cars, machines) *rosak*

break off, to *putus*

break up, divorce *cerai*

break, shatter *pecah, pecahkan, memecahkan*

bridge *jambatan*

bring, to *bawa, membawa*

broad, spacious *luas*

broadcast, programme *siaran*

broadcast, to *siarkan, menyiarkan*

broken off *putus*

broken, does not work, spoiled *rosak*

broken, shattered *pecah*

broken, snapped (of bones, etc.) *patah*

broom *sapu, penyapu*

broth, soup *sup*

brother, older *abang*

brother, younger *adik*

brother-in-law *abang/adik ipar*

brown *coklat*

brush *berus*

brush, to *memberus, menggonyoh*

buffalo *kerbau*

build, to *bangun, membangun*

building *bangunan*

burn, burnt *bakar*

burned down, out *terbakar*

bus *bas*

bus station *stesen bas*

business *bisnis, perniagaan, perdagangan*

businessman *pedagang, peniaga*

busy, crowded *ramai, sibuk*

busy, to be *sibuk*

but *tetapi*

butter *mentega*

butterfly *kupu-kupu, rama-rama*

buy *beli, membeli*

C

cabbage *kobis*

cake, pastry *kuih, kek*

call on the telephone *menelefon*

call, summon *panggil, memanggil*

calm *tenang*

can, be able to *boleh*

can, tin *tin*

cancel *batal, membatalkan*

candle *lilin*

candy, sweet *gula-gula*

capable of, to be *sanggup*

capture, to *tangkap, menangkap*

car, automobile *kereta*

card *kad*

care for, love *sayang, mencintai*

care of, to take *mengasuh, mengawasi*

careful! *hati-hati! awas!*

carrot *keret, lobak merah*

carry, to *bawa, membawa*

cart (buffalo) *kereta lembu*

cart (pushcart) *kereta tolak*

carve, to *ukir, mengukir*

carving *ukiran*

cash money *wang tunai*

cash a check, to *melunaskan cek*

cast, throw out *buang, membuang*

cat *kucing*

catch, to *tangkap, menangkap*

cauliflower *bunga kobis*

cave *gua*

celebrate, to *merayakan*

celery *sayur saderi*

center *pusat, tengah*

central *pusat*

ceremony *upacara*

certain *pasti, tentu*

certainly! *memang!*

chain *rantai*

chair *kerusi*

challenge *cabaran*

champion *juara*

chance, to have an opportunity to *peluang, sempat*

chance, by accident *kebetulan*

chance, opportunity *peluang, kesempatan*

change, small *wang kecil*

change, to (conditions, situations, one's mind) *berubah*

change, exchange (money, opinions) *tukar, menukar*

change, switch (clothes, things) *ganti, mengganti*

character *watak*

characteristic *sifat*

chase away, chase out *usir, mengusir, halau*

chase, to *kejar, mengejar*

cheap *murah*

cheat, someone who cheats *penipu*

cheat, to *tipu, menipu*

cheek *pipi*

cheese *keju*

chess *catur*

chest (box) *peti*

chest (breast) *dada*

chicken *ayam*

child *anak*

chilli pepper *lada, cili*

chilli sauce *sos cili*

chocolate *coklat*

choice *pilihan*

choose, to *pilih, memilih*

church *gereja*

cigarette *rokok*

cinema *pawagam*

citizen *warganegara*

citrus *limau*

city *kota, bandaraya*

clarification *penjelasan*

clarify, to *menjelaskan*

class, category *kelas, kategori*

classes (at university) *kuliah*

clean *bersih*

clean, to *bersihkan, membersihkan, buat bersih*

cleanliness *kebersihan*

clear *jelas, terang*

clear (of weather) *cerah, terang*

clever *cerdik, pandai*

climate *iklim*

climb onto, into *naik*

climb up (of hills, mountains) *mendaki*

clock *jam*

close together, tight *rapat*

close to, nearby *dekat*

close, to cover *menutup*

closed *tutup*

cloth *kain*

clothes, clothing *pakaian*

cloudy, overcast *mendung*

clove *cengkih*

clove cigarette *kretek*

coarse, to be *kasar*

coconut *kelapa*

coffee *kopi*

cold, flu *selsema*

cold *sejuk*

colleague *rakan*

collect payment *menagih bayaran*

color *warna*

comb *sisir, sikat*

come in, to *masuk*

come on, let's go *ayuh, mari*

come, to *datang*

command, order *perintah*

command, to *perintah, memerintah*

company *syarikat*

compare, to *membandingkan*

compared to *dibandingkan*

compatible *cocok, sesuai*

compete, to *bertanding*

competition *pertandingan*

complain, to *bersungut,
mengadu*

complaint *sungutan, aduan*

complete, finish something
*selesaikan,
menyelesaikan*

complete, to be *lengkap*

complete, to make *lengkapi,
melengkapi*

completed, finished *selesai,
siap*

complicated *rumit*

compose, write (letters, books,
music) *karang,
mengarang*

composition, writings
karangan

concerning *tentang,
mengenai*

condition (pre-condition)
syarat

condition (status) *pangkat*

confidence *keyakinan, yakin*

confidence, to have *percaya*

confuse, to *keliru*

confused (in a mess) *kacau,
selarak*

confused (mentally) *bingung*

confusing *membingungkan*

congratulations! *tahniah!*

connect together, to
sambung, menyambung

connection *hubungan,
sambungan*

conscious of, to be *sedari,
menyedari*

conscious *sedar*

consider (to have an opinion)
anggap, menganggap

consider (to think over)
*timbangkan,
pertimbangkan*

consult, talk over with *run-
dingkan, merundingkan*

contact, connection
hubungan

contact, get in touch with
hubungi, menghubungi

continue, to *teruskan,
meneruskan*

cook, to *masak, memasak*

cooked, ripe *masak, matang*

cookie *biskut, kuih*

cooking, cuisine *masakan*

cool *sejuk, dingin*

coral rock *batu karang*

corn *jagung*

cost (expense) *kos, biaya*

cost (price) *harga*

cotton *kapas*

cough *batuk*

count, reckon *hitung,
menghitung*

counter, window (for paying
money, buying tickets)
kaunter

country *negara*

cover, to *tutup, menutup*

crab *ketam, kepiting*

cracked *retak*

cracker, bisquit *biskut*

craft *kraf*

craftsman *tukang*

crate *peti*
crazy *gila*
criminal *penjahat*
crowded *ramai*
cruel *kejam*
cry out, to *teriak, berteriak*
cry, to *tangis, menangis*
cucumber *timun*
culture *kebudayaan*
cup *cawan*
cured,well *sembuh*
custom, tradition *adat*
customer *pelanggan*
cut, slice *potongan*
cut, to *potong, memotong*

D

dance *tarian*
dance, to *tari, menari*
danger *bahaya*
dangerous *berbahaya*
daring, brave *berani*
dark *gelap*
date (of the month) *tarikh*
daughter *anak perempuan*
daughter-in-law *menantu*
day *hari*
day after tomorrow *lusa*
daybreak *fajar*
dazed, dizzy *pusing, pening*
dead *mati*
debt *hutang*
deceive, to *tipu, menipu*
December *Disember*
decide, to *memutuskan*
decision *keputusan*

decrease, to *kurang, berkurangan, mengurangi*
deer *rusa*
defeat, to *kalahkan, mengalahkan*
defecate, to *buang air besar, berak*
defect *cacat*
degree, level *tahap*
degrees (temperature) *darjah*
delicious *sedap, enak*
demand, to *tuntut, menuntut*
depart, to *berangkat, pergi*
depend on, to *bergantung*
deposit, leave behind with someone *deposit, meninggalkan*
deposit, put money in the bank *simpan wang*
describe, to *gambarkan, menggambarkan*
desire *hasrat, nafsu*
desire, to *ingin, mahu*
destination *destinasi*
destroy, to *hancurkan, menghancurkan*
destroyed, ruined *hancur*
determined *nekad*
develop, to *berkembang*
develop, to (film) *cuci, mencuci*
development *kemajuan, perkembangan*
diamond *intan*
dictionary *kamus*
die, to *mati, meninggal*
difference (discrepancy in figures) *perbezaan, selisih*

discrepancy *selisih, percanggahan*

different, other *lain*

difficult *sukar, sulit, susah*

dipper, ladle *gayung*

direct, non-stop *langsung*

direction *jurusan, arah*

dirt, filth *kotoran*

dirty *kotor*

disaster, disastrous *celaka*

discrepancy *selisih*

discuss, to *bicara, membicarakan*

discussion *pembicaraan*

display *pamer*

display, to *mempamerkan*

distance *jarak*

disturb, to *ganggu, mengganggu*

disturbance *gangguan*

divide, split up *bahagi, membahagi*

division *bahagian*

divorce, to *bercerai*

divorced *cerai*

dizzy, ill *pening, sakit*

do not! *jangan!*

do one's best *berusaha, sedaya upaya*

do, perform an action *melakukan*

doctor *doktor*

document, letter *surat*

dog *anjing*

dolphin *ikan lumba-lumba*

done (cooked) *masak, matang*

done (finished) *selesai*

door *pintu*

doubt something, to *ragu-ragu, meragukan*

doubtful *ragu-ragu*

down, to come or go down, get off *turun, menurun*

down, to take down *turunkan, menurunkan*

downtown *pusat bandar*

draw, to *lukis, melukisan*

drawer *laci*

drawing *lukisan*

dream *impian*

dream, to *mimpi, bermimpi*

dress, skirt *baju perempuan*

dressed, to get *berpakaian, ganti baju*

drink, refreshment *minuman*

drink, to *minum*

drive, to (a car) *pandu, memandu*

driver *pemandu*

drowned *tenggelam*

drug, medicine *ubat*

drugstore *farmasi, kedai ubat*

drunk *mabuk*

dry *kering*

dry (weather) *kemarau*

dry out (in the sun) *jemur*

duck *itik*

dusk *senja*

dust *habuk, debu*

duty (import duty) *cukai import/duti import*

duty (responsibility) *kewajipan, tugas, tanggungjawab*

E

each, every **setiap, tiap-tiap**

ear **telinga**

earlier, beforehand **dulu**

early **awal**

early in the morning **pagi-pagi**

Earth, the World **Dunia, bumi**

earth, soil **tanah**

east **timur**

easy **mudah, senang**

eat, to **makan**

echo **gema**

economical **jimat**

economy **ekonomi**

edge **pinggir, tepi, batas**

educate, to **didik, mendidik**

education **pendidikan**

effort **usaha**

effort, to make an **berusaha**

egg **telur**

eggplant **terong**

eight **lapan**

electric, electricity **elektrik**

elephant **gajah**

eleven **sebelas**

embarrassed **malu**

embarrassing **memalukan**

embassy **kedutaan besar**

emergency **darurat, kecemasan**

empty **kosong**

end, tip **hujung**

enemy **musuh**

energy **tenaga**

enlarge, to **besarkan, membesarkan**

enough **cukup**

enter, to **masuk**

entire **seluruh**

entirety, whole **keseluruhan**

envelope **sampul**

envy, envious **iri hati, cemburu**

equal **sama**

equality **kesamaan**

especially **khusus**

establish, set up **mendirikan**

estimate, to **taksir, menafsir**

ethnic group **bangsa, suku bangsa**

even (also) **juga**

even (smooth) **rata**

ever, have already **pernah**

every kind of **segala macam**

every **tiap, segala**

every time **tiap kali**

exact, exactly **tepat**

exactly! just so! **betul!**

exam, test **ujian, periksaan**

examine, to **periksa, memeriksa**

example **contoh, misalan**

example, for **misalnya**

except **kecuali**

exchange rate **kadar petukaran**

exchange, to (money, opinions) **tukar, menukar**

excuse me! **ma'af!**

exit **keluar**

expand, grow larger **mengembang**

expect, to **harapkan, mengharapkan**

expect, to **mengharap**

expense **biaya**

expensive *mahal*

expert *pakar*

express, state *ucapkan, mengucapkan*

extend, to *perpanjang, memperpanjangkan*

extremely *sangat*

eye *mata*

eyeglasses *kacamata*

F

face *muka*

face, to *hadapi, menghadapi*

fail, to *gagal*

failure *kegagalan*

fall (season) *musim gugur*

fall, to *jatuh*

false (imitation) *palsu*

false (not true) *keliru*

falsify, to *tiru, meniru, palsukan*

family *keluarga*

fan (admirer) *peminat*

fan (used for cooling) *kipas*

fancy *mewah, menarik*

far *jauh*

fart, to *kentut*

fast *cepat, lekas*

fat, grease *lemak*

fat, to be *gemuk*

father *bapa, ayah*

father-in-law *bapa mertua*

fault, to *salahkan, menyalahkan*

fear *takut*

February *Februari*

feel, to *rasa, merasa*

feeling *perasaan, rasa*

fertile *subur*

fever *demam*

field, empty space *padang, kawasan lapang*

fierce *garang, galak*

fight over, to *berebut*

fight, to (physically) *lawan*

fill, to *isi, mengisi*

film *filem*

filter *saringan, tapis*

filter, to *saring, menyaring, menapis*

find, to *cari, mencari*

finger *jari*

fingernail *kuku*

finish off, to *habiskan, selesaikan*

finish *selesaikan, menyelesaikan*

finished (completed) *selesai*

finished (no more) *habis*

fire *api*

fire someone, to *pecat, memecat*

first *pertama*

first, earlier, beforehand *terdahalu*

fish *ikan*

fish, to *pancing, memancing*

fit, to *sesuai, muat*

fitting, suitable *cocok, sesuai*

five *lima*

fix, to (a time, appointment) *menentukan*

fix, to (repair) *betulkan, membetulkan*

flag *bendera*

flood *banjir*

floor *lantai*
flour *tepung*
flower *bunga, kembang*
flu *selsema, demam*
fluent *lancar, fasih*
flute *seruling*
fly (insect) *lalat*
fly, to *terbang, menerbang*
follow along, to *ikut*
follow behind, to *menyusul*
following *berikut*
fond of, to be *sayang, menyayangi*
food *makanan*
foot *kaki*
for *untuk, bagi*
forbid, to *melarang*
forbidden *dilarang, larangan*
force *daya*
force, to *paksa, memaksa*
foreign *asing*
foreigner *orang asing*
forest *hutan*
forget about, to *melupakan*
forget, to *lupa*
forgive, to *mengampuni*
forgiveness, mercy *ampun*
forgotten *terlupa*
fork *garpu*
form (shape) *bentuk, rupa*
form (to fill out) *melengkapkan*
fortress *benteng, kubu, kota*
four *empat*
free of charge *percuma*
free of restraints *bebas*
free, independent *merdeka*
freedom *kemerdekaan*

fresh *segar*
Friday *Jumaat*
fried *goreng*
friend *kawan, teman*
friendly, outgoing *ramah*
from *dari*
front *depan, muka*
fruit *buah*
fry, to *goreng, menggoreng*
full *penuh*
full, eaten one's fill *kenyang*
fullfill, to *penuhi, memenuhi*
function, to work *jalan, berjalan*
funds, funding *dana*
fungus *cendawan*
funny *lucu, jenaka*

G

gamble *judi, berjudi*
garage (for repairs) *bengkel*
garage (for keeping a car) *garej*
garbage *sampah*
garden *taman, kebun*
garlic *bawang putih*
gasoline *minyak petrol*
gasoline station *setesen minyak*
gather, to *kumpul, mengumpul*
gender *kelamin, jantina*
general, all-purpose *umum*
generally *pada umumnya*
gentle *lembut*
get, receive *dapat, mendapat*
ghost *hantu*

gift *hadiah*

girl *gadis, anak perempuan*

give *beri, memberi*

glass (for drinking) *gelas*

glass (material) *kaca*

go along, join in *ikut, mengikuti*

go around *keliling*

go back *balik*

go down, get off *turun*

go for a walk *jalan-jalan*

go home *pulang*

go out, exit *keluar*

go *pergi, jalan*

go up, climb *naik*

goal *tujuan*

goat *kambing*

God *Tuhan*

god *dewa*

goddess *dewi*

gold *emas*

gone, finished *habis*

good *baik, bagus*

government *pemerintah, kerajaan*

grand, great *hebat*

grandchild *cucu*

grandfather *datuk*

grandmother *nenek*

grape *anggur*

grass *rumput*

grave *kubur, makam*

gray *warna kelabu*

great, formidable *hebat*

green *hijau*

green (French) beans *kacang buncis*

greet, to receive *sambut, menyambut*

greetings *salam*

grill, to *panggang, memanggang*

grow larger, to *berkembang, membesar*

grow, to (intransitive) *tumbuh, bertumbuh*

grow, plant *tanam, menanam*

guarantee *jaminan*

guarantee, to *jamin, menjamin*

guard, to *jaga, menjaga*

guess, to *teka*

guest *tetamu*

guide, lead *bimbing*

guidebook *buku panduan*

H

hair *rambut*

half *setengah, separuh*

hall *ruang*

hand (also wrist, forearm) *tangan*

handicap *cacat*

handicraft *kraftangan*

handsome *kacak, lawa*

hang, to *gantung, menggantung*

happen, occur *terjadi*

happened, what happened? *apa yang terjadi?*

happening, incident *kejadian*

happy *bahagia, gembira*

hard (difficult) *sukar, susah*

hard (solid) *keras*

hardworking, industrious *rajin*

harmonious *rukun*

hat *topi*

have been, ever *pernah*

have, own, belong to *punya*

he *dia*

head *kepala*

healthy *sihat*

hear, to *dengar*

heart *hati, jantung*

heavy *berat*

help, to *tolong, menolong; bantu, membantu*

her *dia*

here *sini, di sini*

hidden *tersembunyi*

hide, to *menyembunyikan*

high *tinggi*

hill *bukit*

him *dia*

hinder, to *menghalang*

hindrance *halangan*

history *sejarah*

hit, strike *pukul, memukul*

hold back, to *tahan, bertahan*

hold onto, grasp *pegang, memegang*

hole *lubang*

holiday *cuti*

holy *keramat*

home, house *rumah*

honey *madu*

hope, to *harap, berharap*

horse *kuda*

hospital *hospital/rumah sakit*

hot (spicy) *pedas*

hot (temperature) *panas*

hot spring *mata air panas*

hour *jam*

house *rumah*

how are you? *apa khabar?*

how many? *berapa banyak?*

how much? *berapa?*

how? *bagaimana?*

human *manusia*

humane *kemanusiaan*

humorous *lucu, jenaka*

hundred *ratus*

hungry *lapar*

hurt (injured) *luka*

hurt (to cause pain) *sakit*

husband *suami*

hut, shack *pondok*

I

I *saya*

ice *ais*

if *kalau, jika*

imagine, to *bayangkan, membayangkan*

importance, important matters *kepentingan*

important *penting*

impossible *tidak mungkin*

impression *kesan, tanggapan*

impression, to make an *memberi kesan*

in (time, years) *pada*

in order that, so that *agar, supaya*

in, at (space) *di*

included, including *termasuk*

increase, to **bertambah, tambah banyak**

indeed! **memang!**

indigenous **asli**

influence **pengaruh**

influence, to **mempengaruhi**

influenza **selsema**

inform, to **terangkan, beritahu, memberitahukan**

information **keterangan**

information booth **pondok penerangan**

inhale, to **hisap**

inject, to **menyuntik, suntik**

injection **suntikan**

injury, injured **luka, kecederaan**

inside **dalam**

inside of **di dalam**

inspect, to **periksa, memeriksa**

instruct, send to do something **suruh, menyuruh**

insult **cacian**

insult someone, to **mencaci**

insurance **insurans**

intend, to **hendak, bermaksud**

intended for **ditujukan kepada**

intention **maksud**

interest (paid to pr by a bank) **faedah**

interesting **menarik**

intersection **persimpangan**

into **ke dalam**

invitation **undangan**

invite, to (ask along) **jemput**

invite, to (formally) **jemputan**

involve, to **melibatkan**

involved **terlibat**

iron **besi**

iron, to (clothing) **gosok, menggosok**

is **adalah, merupakan**

island **pulau**

it **ini, itu**

item **barang**

ivory **gading**

J

jail **penjara**

jam **jem**

January **Januari**

jealous **cemburu**

job **pekerjaan, tugas**

join together, to **sambung, gabung**

join, go along **ikut, mengikuti**

journalist **wartawan**

July **Julai**

jump, to **lompat, melompat**

June **Jun**

jungle **hutan**

just now **baru saja, baru tadi**

just, only **cuma, hanya, saja**

K

keep, to **simpan, menyimpan**

key **kunci**

kill, murder **membunuh**

kind, good (of persons) **baik hati**

kind, type **macam, jenis**

king **raja**

kiss *cium, mencium*

kitchen *dapur*

knife *pisau*

knock, to *ketuk, mengetuk*

know, to *tahu*

know, be acquainted with *kenal, mengenal*

knowledge *pengetahuan*

L

ladle, dipper *gayung*

lady *perempuan*

lake *tasik, danau*

lamb, mutton *daging kambing*

lamp *lampu*

land *tanah*

land, to (a plane) *mendarat*

lane *lorong*

language *bahasa*

large *besar*

last night *tadi*

last *terakhir*

late at night *malam-malam*

late *lewar malam*

later *kemudian*

laugh at, to *ketawakan, menertawakan*

laugh, to *tertawa, ketawa*

lavish, fancy *mewah*

laws, legislation *undang-undang, hukum*

layer *lapisan*

lazy *malas*

lead (to be a leader) *memimpin*

lead (to guide someone somewhere) *hantar, menghantar*

leader *pemimpin*

leaf *daun*

leather *kulit*

leave behind by accident *ketinggalan*

leave behind on purpose *tinggalkan, meninggalkan*

leave behind for safekeeping *simpan*

leave, depart *pergi, berangkat*

lecture *kuliah, bersyarah*

lecturer (at university) *pensyarah*

left side *kiri*

leg (also foot) *kaki*

lend, to *pinjamkan, meminjamkan*

less *kurang*

lessen, reduce *mengurangkan*

lesson *pelajaran*

let someone know, to *beritahu, kasih tahu*

let, allow *biar, membiarkan*

letter *surat*

level (even, flat) *rata*

level (height) *ketinggian*

level (standard) *nilai*

license (for driving) *lesen pemandu*

license, permit *lesen*

lie down, to *baring, tidur*

lie, tell a falsehood *bohong*

life *nyawa*

lifetime *kehidupan*

lift *angkat, mengangkat*

light (bright) *terang*

light (lamp) *lampu*
light bulb *mentol*
lightning *kilat*
lightweight *ringan*
like, as *macam*
like, be pleased by *senang, suka*
line *garisan*
line up, to *beratur*
list *daftar*
listen *dengar, mendengar*
listen to *dengarkan, mendengarkan*
literature *sastra, kesusasteraan*
little (not much) *sedikit*
little (small) *kecil*
live (stay in a place) *tinggal*
live (be alive) *hidup*
liver *hati*
load *muatan*
load up, to *muat, memuat*
lock *kunci*
lock, to *mengunci*
locked *terkunci, dikunci*
lodge, small hotel *penginapan, rumah tumpangan*
lonely *kesepian*
long (time) *lama*
long (length) *panjang*
look after, to *mengawasi, menjaga*
look for, to *cari, mencari*
look out! *awas!*
look, see *lihat, melihat*
lose money, to *rugi*
lose something, to *hilang, kehilangan*

lose, be defeated *kalah*
lost (of things) *hilang*
lost (to lose one's way) *sesat*
love *cinta, sayang*
love, to *mencintai*
low *rendah*
loyal *setia*
luck *nasib baik*
luggage *beg*

M

madam *puan*
magazine *majalah*
make, to *buat, membuat*
male *laki-laki*
man *orang lelaki*
manufacture, to *buatkan*
many, much *banyak*
map *peta*
March *Mac*
marijuana *ganja*
market *pasar*
market, to *pasarkan, memasarkan*
married *kahwin, nikah*
marry, get married *menikah, berkahwin*
mask *topeng*
massage *picit, urut*
massage, to *mengurut*
mat *tikar*
material, ingredient *bahan*
matter, issue *soal, hal*
mattress *tilam*
May *Mei*
may *boleh*

maybe *mungkin*

me *saya*

mean (to intend to) *bermaksud*

mean (cruel) *kejam, bengis*

mean, to *bererti*

meaning *erti, maksud*

measure, to *ukur, mengukur*

measurement *ukuran*

meat *daging*

medicine *ubat*

meet, to *bertemu, ketemu, jumpa, berjumpa, menjumpai*

meeting *pertemuan, mesyuarat*

member *ahli, anggota*

memories *kenang-kenangan*

mention, to *menyebutkan*

mentioned *tersebut*

menu *menu*

mercy *ampun*

merely *cuma, hanya*

message *pesanan*

metal *logam, besi*

method *cara*

meticulous *teliti*

middle, center *tengah*

middle, be in the middle of *sedang, ditengah*

milk *susu*

million *juta*

mirror *cermin*

mix, mixed *campur*

modest, simple *sederhana*

moment (in a moment, just a moment) *sekejap, sebentar*

moment (instant) *saat*

Monday *Isnin*

money *wang, duit*

monkey *monyet, kera*

month, moon *bulan*

monument *tugu*

moon, month *bulan*

more (comparative quality) *lebih*

more of (things) *lagi, lebih banyak*

morning *pagi*

mosque *masjid*

mosquito netting *kelambu*

mosquito *nyamuk*

most (the most of) *paling banyak, terbanyak*

most (superlative) *paling*

most, at most *paling-paling*

mother *ibu*

mother-in-law *ibu mertua*

motorcycle *motorsikal*

mountain *gunung*

mouse, rat *tikus*

moustache *misai*

mouth *mulut*

move from one place to another *pindah, memindahkan*

move, to *gerak, bergerak*

movement, motion *gerakan*

movie theater *pawagam*

much, many *banyak*

mushroom *cendawan*

must *mesti*

mutton *daging kambing*

mutual, mutually *saling*

my, mine *saya, saya punya*

N

nail (fingernail) *kuku*
nail (spike) *paku*
naked *telanjang*
name *nama*
narrow *sempit*
nation, country *negara*
nation, people *bangsa*
national *kebangsaan*
nationality *kewarga negaraan*
natural *semulajadi*
nature *alam*
naughty *nakal*
nearby *dekat*
neat, orderly *rapi, teratur*
necessary, must *perlu, mesti*
neck *leher*
need *keperluan, kebutuhan*
need, to *perlu, butuh*
needle *jarum*
neighbor *jiran, tetangga*
nephew, niece *anak saudara*
nest *sarang*
net *jaring*
network *jaringan*
never *tidak pernah*
new *baru*
news *kabar, khabar*
newspaper *surat khabar*
next (in line, sequence) *berikut*
next to *di samping, di sebelah*
niece, nephew *anak saudara*
night *malam*
nightly *tiap malam*
nine *sembilan*

no, not (of nouns) *bukan*
no, not (of verbs and adjectives) *tidak*
noise *bunyi*
noisy *bising*
non-stop *terus, tidak berhenti*
nonsense *karut*
noodles *mee*
noon *tengah hari*
normal *biasa*
normally *biasanya*
north *utara*
nose *hidung*
not *tidak, bukan*
not yet *belum*
note down, to *mencatat*
notes *catatan*
novel *novel*
November *November*
now *sekarang*
nude *telanjang, bogel*
number *nombor*

O

o'clock *pukul, jam*
obey, to *turut, menurut*
occupation *pekerjaan*
ocean *laut, samudra*
October *Oktober*
odor, bad smell *bau*
of, from *dari*
off, to turn off *menutup*
off, turned off *ditutup*
office *pejabat*
official, formal *rasmi*

officials (government) *pegawai*

often *sering, selalu*

oil *minyak*

old (of persons) *tua*

old (of things) *lama, tua*

older sister *kakak*

older brother *abang*

on (of dates) *pada*

on time *pada waktu*

on, at *di*

on, to turn on *hidupkan, jalankan*

on, turned on *hidup, jalan*

once *sekali*

one *satu, se-*

one who, the one which *yang*

onion *bawang*

only *sahaja, cuma, hanya*

open *buka, terbuka*

open, to *membuka*

opponent *lawan, pesaing*

opportunity *kesempatan*

oppose, to *melawan*

opposed, in opposition *berlawanan, bertentangan*

or *atau*

orange *oren*

order (command) *perintah*

order (placed for food, goods) *pesanan*

order (sequence) *urutan*

order something, to *pesan*

order, to be in sequence *berturutan*

order, to command *perintah, memerintah*

orderly, organized *teratur, rapi*

organize, arrange *mengatur, mengurus, menyelenggarakan*

origin *asal*

original *asli*

originate, come from *berasal dari*

other *lain*

out *luar*

out, go out *keluar*

outside *luar, di luar*

over, finished *selesai*

over, to turn *balik*

overcast, cloudy *mendung*

overcome, to *mengatasi*

overseas *luar negeri*

overturned *terbalik*

own, to *memiliki, mempunyai*

oyster *tiram*

P

pack, to *membungkus*

package *bungkusan*

paid *sudah bayar*

painful *sakit*

paint *cat*

paint, to (a painting) *melukis*

paint, to (houses, furniture) *cat, mengecat*

painting *lukisan*

pair of, a *sepasang*

palace *istana*

panorama *pemandangan*

pants *seluar*

paper *kertas*

parcel *bungkusan*

pardon me? what did you say?
cuba ulangi?

parents *orang tua, ibubapa*

part *bahagian*

participate *menyertai*

particularly, especially
khususnya, terkhusus

party *pesta*

pass away, die *meninggal*

passenger *penumpang*

past *melalui, masa silam*

patient (calm) *sabar*

patient (doctor's) *pesakit*

pay, to *bayar, membayar*

payment *pembayaran*

peace *perdamaian*

peaceful *damai*

peak, summit *puncak*

peanut *kacang tanah*

peel, to *kupas, mengupas*

penetrate, to *tembus,
menembus*

people *rakyat*

pepper, black *lada hitam*

pepper, chilli *cabai, cili, lada*

percent, percentage *peratus*

performance *pertunjukan*

perhaps, maybe *mungkin*

perhaps, probably *barangkali*

period (end of a sentence)
titik, noktah

period (of time) *jangka
waktu, masa waktu*

permanent *tetap*

permit, license *lesen*

permit, to allow *mengizinkan*

person *orang*

personality *watak*

pharmacy *farmasi*

pick up, to (someone)
jemput, menjemput

pick up, lift (something)
angkat, mengangkat

pick, choose *pilih, memilih*

pickpocket *penyeluk saku*

pickpocket, to *menyeluk saku*

piece, portion, section
bahagian

pierce, penetrate *tembus,
menembus*

pig, pork *babi*

pillow *bantal*

pineapple *nanas*

pity! what a pity! *sayang!*

place *tempat*

place, put *taruh, tempatkan,
menempatkan, letak*

plan *rancangan*

plan, to *merancangkan*

plant *tanaman*

plant, to *tanam*

plate *piring*

play around *main-main*

play, to *main, memain*

please (go ahead) *sila*

please (request for help) *tolong*

please (request for something)
minta

pocket *kocek, saku*

point (in time) *saat*

point out, to *menunjuk*

point, dot *detik*

poison, poisonous *racun, bisa*

police *polis*

pond *kolam*

pool *kolam*

poor *miskin*

pork, pig *babi*

porpoise *ikan lumba-lumba*

possible *mungkin*

post, column *tiang*

postpone, to *tunda, menunda*

postponed, delayed *tertunda, ditunda*

potato *ubi kentang*

pour, to *tuangkan, menuangkan*

power *kuasa, kekuasaan, kekuatan*

powerful *berkuasa, kuat*

practice *latihan*

practice, to *berlatih, melatih*

prawn *udang*

pray, to *berdoa, sembahyang*

prayer *doa*

pregnant *hamil*

prejudice *prasangka*

prepare, to make ready *siapkan*

prepared, ready *siap*

prescription *preskripsi*

present moment, at the *pada saat ini, sekarang*

presently, nowadays *sekarang, kini*

press, journalism *pihak akhbar, kewartawanan*

press, to *tekan, menekan*

pressure *tekanan*

pretty (of places, things) *indah*

pretty (of women) *cantik*

pretty, very *agak, sangat*

price *harga*

priest *paderi*

print *cetak*

private *sulit*

probably *barangkali*

problem *masalah*

produce *buat, menghasilkan, mengeluarkan*

profit, luck *untung*

program, schedule *acara*

promise, to *janji, berjanji*

proof *bukti*

prove, to *membuktikan*

public *umum*

publish, to *menerbitkan*

pull, to *tarik, menarik*

pump *pam*

pure *sempurna, tulin*

purse *beg duit*

push, to *dorong, mendorong, tolak*

put into, inside *masukkan, memasukkan*

put together, to *pasang, memasang*

put, to place *taruh, menaruh, letak, meletak*

Q

quarter *suku*

queen *ratu*

question *pertanyaan, soalan*

question, to *tanyakan, menanyakan, menyoal*

queue up *beratur*

quiet *sepi, sunyi*

quite *agak*

R

rain *hujan*

rain, to *hujan*

raise, lift *angkat*

rank, station in life *pangkat*

ranking *kedudukan, tahap*

rare (scarce) *jarang*

rare (uncooked) *mentah, setengah masak*

rarely, seldom *jarang*

rat *tikus*

rate of exchange (for foreign currency) *kadar pertukaran*

rate, tariff *tarif, tambang*

rather *agak*

rather than *daripada*

raw, uncooked, rare *mentah, setengah masak*

ray *sinar*

reach *sampai, mencapai*

react, to *bertindakbalas*

reaction *tindakbalas*

read *baca, membaca*

ready *siap*

ready, to get *bersiap*

ready, to make *siapkan, menyiapkan*

realize, be aware of *sedari, menyedari*

really! *sungguh!*

rear, tail *ekor, belakang*

receive *terima, menerima*

recipe *resipi*

recognize, to *kenal, mengenal*

recovered, cured *sembuh*

red *merah*

reduce, to *kurangi, mengurangi*

refined *bersih, halus*

reflect, to *mencerminkan*

refuse, to *tolak, menolak*

regarding *terhadap, mengenai*

region *daerah*

register, to *daftar, mendaftar*

registered post *pos berdaftar*

registered *berdaftar*

regret, to *menyesal*

regular, normal *biasa*

relax *bersantai, berehat*

release, to *lepas, melepaskan*

released *terlepas, dilepas*

religion *agama*

remainder, leftover *sisa*

remains (historical) *peninggalan*

remember, to *ingat*

remembrances *kenang-kenangan*

remind, to *mengingatkan*

rent out, to *sewakan, menyewakan*

repair, to *membetulkan, memperbaiki*

repaired *betul, perbaiki*

repeat, to *ulang, mengulangi*

reply, response *balasan, jawapan*

reply, to (in writing or deeds) *membalas*

reply, to (verbally) *menjawab*

report *laporan*

report, to *lapor, melapor*

request, to (formally) *mohon, memohon*

request, to (informally) *minta*

research *penyelidikan*

research, to *selidiki, menyelidiki*

reservation *tempahan*

reserve, for animals *taman haiwan*

reserve, to ask for in advance *pesan dulu, tempah*

resident, inhabitant *penduduk*

resolve, to (a problem) *mengatasi, membereskan*

respect *hormat*

respect, to *menghormati*

respond, react *bertindak balas*

response, reaction *tanggapan, tindak balas*

responsibility *tanggungjawab*

responsible, to be *bertanggung jawab*

rest, relax *istirahat*

restrain, to *tahan, tahankan*

restroom *tandas, bilik air*

result *akibat, hasil*

resulting from, as a result of *disebabkan oleh, karena*

return home, to *pulang*

return (to give back) *mengembalikan*

return (go back) *kembali, balik*

reverse, back up *mundur*

reversed, backwards *terbalik*

rice (cooked) *nasi*

rice (plant) *padi*

rice (uncooked grains) *beras*

ricefields *sawah*

rich *kaya*

rid, get rid of *membuang, menghilangkan*

ride, mount, climb *naik*

right, correct *betul, benar*

right-hand side *kanan*

rights *hak*

ring *cincin*

ripe *matang, masak*

river *sungai*

road *jalan*

roast, grill *panggang*

roasted, grilled, toasted *bakar, panggang*

role *peranan*

room *bilik*

root *akar*

rope *tali*

rotten *busuk*

rough *kasar*

run, to *lari*

S

sacred *keramat*

sacrifice *korban*

sacrifice, to *mengorbankan*

sad *sedih*

safe *selamat*

sail *layar*

sail, to *berlayar*

salary *gaji*

sale *penjualan*

sale (at reduced prices) *lelong*

salt *garam*

salty *masin*

same *sama*

sample *contoh*

sand *pasir*

satisfied *puas*

satisfy, to *memuaskan*

Saturday *Sabtu*

sauce *sos*

sauce (chilli paste) *sambal*

save money, to *menjimatkan*

save, keep *simpan*

say, to *berkata, mengatakan cakap, bercakap*

scarce *jarang, sedikit*

schedule *jadual waktu*

school *sekolah*

science *sains, ilmu*

scissors *gunting*

scrub, to *gosok, menggosok*

sculpt, to *pahat, memahat*

sculpture *ukiran*

sea *laut*

search for, to *cari, mencari*

season *musim*

seat *tempat duduk*

second *kedua*

secret *rahasia*

secret, to keep a *rahasiakan*

secretary *setiausaha*

secure, safe *aman, selamat*

see, to (also observe, visit, read) *lihat, melihat*

seed *biji*

seek, to *cari, mencari*

select, to *pilih, memilih*

self *diri, sendiri*

sell, to *jual, menjual*

send, to *kirim, mengirim*

sentence *kalimat, ayat*

separate, to *pisah, memisahkan*

September *September*

sequence, order *urutan*

serious (not funny) *serius*

serious, severe (of problems, illnesses, etc.) *parah*

servant *pelayan, pembantu*

serve, to *melayani*

service *perkhidmatan*

seven *tujuh*

severe (of problems, illnesses, etc.) *parah*

sew, to *jahit, menjahit*

sex, gender *kelamin*

shack *pondok*

shadow *bayang*

shadow play *wayang kulit*

shake, to (intransitive) *goyang, bergoyang*

shake something, to (transitive) *goncang*

shall, will *akan*

shape *bentuk*

shape, to form *membentuk*

sharp *tajam*

shatter, to *pecahkan, memecahkan*

shattered *pecah*

shave, to *cukur, mencukur*

she *dia (perempuan)*

sheep *kambing biri-biri*

ship *kapal*

shirt *baju*

shit *berak*

shoes *kasut*

shop, store *kedai*

shop, go shopping *belanja, berbelanja, membeli-belah*

short (concise) *ringkas, pendek*

short (not tall) *pendek*

short time, a moment *sekejap, sebentar*

shoulder *bahu*

shout, to *teriak, berteriak*

show, broadcast *siaran*

show, live performance *pertunjukan*

show, to *menunjukkan, memperlihatkan*

shrimp, prawn *udang*

shut *tutup, menutupi*

sick *sakit*

side *samping, tepi*

sign, symbol *tanda, simbol*

sign, to *tanda tangani, menanda tangani*

signature *tanda tangan*

signboard *papan tanda*

silent, quiet *diam, sepi*

silk *sutera*

silver *perak*

simple (easy) *senang, mudah*

simple (uncomplicated, modest) *sederhana*

since *sejak*

sinews *urat*

sing, to *nyanyi, bernyanyi*

sir *tuan*

sister (older) *kakak*
  (younger) *adik perempuan*

sister-in-law *ipar perempuan*

sit down, to *duduk*

six *enam*

sixteen *enam belas*

sixty *enam puluh*

size *ukuran, kebesaran*

skewer *pencucuk daging*

skin *kulit*

sky *langit*

sleep, to *tidur*

sleepy *mengantuk*

slow *lambat, perlahan*

slowly *perlahan-perlahan*

small *kecil*

smart *pandai, pintar*

smell, bad odor *bau, bau busuk*

smell, to *cium, mencium*

smile, to *senyum, bersenyum*

smoke *asap*

smoke, to (tobacco) *rokok, merokok*

smooth (to go smoothly) *lancar*

smooth (of surfaces) *rata*

smuggle, to *seludup, menyeludup*

snake *ular*

snow *salji*

snowpeas *kacang kapri*

so that *agar, supaya*

so very *begitu*

soap *sabun*

socks *stoking pendek*

soft *empuk, lunak*

sold out *habis*

sold *terjual, laku*

sole, only *tunggal, satu-satunya*

solve, to (a problem) **menye-lesaikan, membereskan**

solved, resolved **menyelesaikan**

some **beberapa**

sometimes **kadang-kadang**

son **anak laki-laki**

son-in-law **menantu lelaki**

song **lagu**

soon **sekejap**

sorry, to feel regretful **menyesal**

sorry! **maaf!**

soul **jiwa**

sound **bunyi**

soup (spicy) **sup**

sour **masam**

source **sumber**

south **selatan**

soy sauce (salty) **kicap**

soy sauce (sweet) **kicap manis**

space **tempat**

spacious **luas, lapang**

speak, to **cakap, bercakap**

special **khusus, istimewa**

speech (oration) **pidato, syarahan**

speed **kecepatan, laju, kelajuan**

spend, to **keluarkan, mengeluarkan**

spices **rempah-rempah**

spinach **bayam, kangkong**

spirit **semangat, nyawa**

spoiled (does not work) **rusak**

spoiled (of food) **busuk**

spoon **sudu**

spray, to **sembur, menyembur**

spring **mata air**

square (shape) **persegi**

square, town square **dataran**

squid **sotong**

stamp (ink) **cap**

stamp (postage) **setem**

stand up, to **berdiri**

star **bintang**

start, to **mula, memulakan**

startled **terkejut**

startling **mengejutkan**

statue **ukiran**

stay overnight, to **bermalam, menginap**

stay, to **tinggal, berdiam**

steal, to **curi, mencuri**

steam **wap**

steamed **kukus**

steel **besi**

step **langkah**

steps, stairs **tangga**

stick out, to **tonjol, menonjol**

stick, pole **batang**

stick to, to **melekat, menempel**

sticky **melekit**

stiff **kaku**

still **masih**

stink, to **bau, berbau**

stomach, belly **perut**

stone **batu**

stop by, to pay a visit **singgah**

stop, to **berhenti, stop**

store **kedai**

store, to **simpan, menyimpan**

story (of a building) **lantai, tingkat**

story (tale) **cerita**

straight (not crooked) *lurus*
straight ahead *terus, lurus*
strait *selat*
street *jalan*
strength *kekuatan*
strict *ketat*
strike, to go on *mogok kerja*
strike, hit *pukul, memukul*
string *tali*
strong *kuat*
struck, hit *kena*
stubborn, determined *nekad, degil*
study, learn *belajar*
stupid *bodoh*
style *gaya*
submerged, drowned *tenggelam*
succeed, to *berhasil*
success *keberhasilan*
suddenly *tiba-tiba*
suffer, to *sengsara*
suffering *kesengsaraan*
sugar *gula*
sugarcane *tebu*
suggest *mengusul, sarankan*
suggestion *usul, saranan*
suitable, fitting, compatible *sesuai, berpadanan*
suitcase *beg pakaian*
summit, peak *puncak*
sun *matahari*
Sunday *Minggu, Ahad*
sunlight *sinar matahari*
supermarket *supermarket, pasar raya*
suppose, to *kira, mengira*
sure *pasti*

surf *ombak*
surface *permukaan*
surprised *hairan*
surprising *menghairankan*
suspect, to *mencuriga, menyangka*
suspicion *kecurigaan*
sweat *peluh, keringat*
sweep, to *sapu, menyapu*
sweet *manis*
swim, to *berenang*
swimming pool *kolam renang*
swimming suit *pakaian renang*
swing, to *goyang, bergoyang*
switch on, turn on *pasang, memasang, nyalakan, hidupkan*
switch, change *ganti, mengganti*

T

t-shirt *baju t*
table *meja*
tail *ekor*
take *ambil, mengambil*
tall *tinggi*
taste *rasa*
tasty *enak*
tea *teh*
teach, to *ajar, mengajar*
teacher *guru*
team *pasukan*
teen *belasan*
teeth *gigi*
tell, to (a story) *menceritakan*

tell, to (let know) **beritahu**

temple (Chinese) **tokong**

temple (Indian) **kuil**

temporary, temporarily **sementara**

ten **sepuluh**

tendon **urat**

tens of, multiples of ten **puluhan**

tense **tegang**

test **ujian**

test, to **uji, menguji**

than **daripada**

thank you **terima kasih**

that (introducing a quotation) **bahwa**

that, those **itu**

that, which, the one who **yang**

theater, cinema **pawagam**

their, theirs **mereka punya**

then **lalu, kemudian, lantas**

there **di sana, di situ**

they, them **mereka**

thick (of liquids) **pekat, kental**

thick (of things) **tebal**

thief **pencuri**

thin (of liquids) **cair**

thin (of persons) **kurus**

thing **barang, benda**

think, to **fikir, berfikir**

third **ketiga**

thirsty **haus**

thirteen **tiga belas**

this, these **ini**

thoughts **fikiran**

thousand **ribu**

thread **benang**

three **tiga**

through, past **lewat, melalui**

throw out, throw away **buang**

thunder **guruh**

Thursday **Khamis**

thus, so **begini, begitu, demikian**

ticket **tiket**

ticket window **loket**

tie, necktie **tali leher**

tie, to **ikat, mengikat**

tiger **harimau**

time to time, once in awhile **kadang-kadang**

time **waktu**

times **kali**

tip (end) **hujung**

tip (gratuity) **hadiah**

tired (sleepy) **mengantuk**

tired (worn out) **letih, penat**

title (of books, films) **judul**

title (of persons) **gelaran**

to, toward (a person) **kepada**

to, toward (a place) **ke**

today **hari ini**

together **bersama-sama, sekalian**

toilet **tandas, bilik air**

tomorrow **besok**

tongue **lidah**

tonight **malam ini**

too (also) **juga**

too (excessive) **terlalu**

too bad **sayang, malangnya**

too much **terlalu banyak**

tool, utensil, instrument **alat**

tooth **gigi**

top **atas**

touch, to *sentuh, menyentuh*

towards *menuju*

towel *tuala*

tower *menara*

town *bandar, kota*

trade, business *perdagangan, perniagaan*

trade, to exchange *tukar, menukar*

train *keretapi*

train station *stesen keretapi*

tree *pokok*

tribe *suku*

trouble *kesusahan*

trouble, to *mengganggu*

troublesome *susah*

true *benar, betul*

truly *bersungguh-sungguh*

try *cuba, mencuba*

Tuesday *Selasa*

turn around *pusing*

turn off, to *mematikan, memadamkan*

turn on, to *nyalakan, pasang*

turn, make a turn *belok, membelok*

turtle (land) *kura-kura*

turtle (sea) *penyu*

twelve *dua belas*

twenty *dua puluh*

two *dua*

type, sort *macam, jenis*

U

ugly *hodoh*

umbrella *payung*

uncle *pak cik*

uncooked *mentah*

under *di bawah*

understand, to *mengerti*

underwear *pakaian dalam*

university *universiti*

unneccessary *tidak usah, tidak perlu*

unripe, young *muda*

until *sampai, hingga*

upside down *terbalik*

upstairs *atas, di atas*

urge, to push for *mendesak*

urinate, to *kencing, buang air kecil*

use, to *pakai, memakai, gunakan, menggunakan*

useful, to be *guna, berguna*

useless *tidak berguna, sia-sia*

usual *biasa*

usually *biasanya, pada umumnya*

V

vaccination *suntikan*

valid *laku, sah*

value *harga*

value, to *hargai, menghargai*

vegetable *sayur*

vegetables *sayuran*

very, extremely *sangat, sekali*

via *melalui*

view, panorama *pemandangan*

view, to look at *memandang*

village *kampung, desa*

vinegar *cuka*

visit *lawatan*
visit, to pay a *melawat*
voice *suara*
volcano *gunung berapi*
vomit, to *muntah*

W

wages *gaji, upah*
wait for, to *tunggu, menunggu*
waiter, waitress *pelayan*
wake someone up *membangunkan*
wake up *bangun, membangun*
walk *jalan, berjalan*
wall *tembok, dinding*
wallet *dompet*
want, to *mahu*
war, battle *peperangan*
war, to make *berperang*
warm *hangat, panas*
warn, to *memberi amaran*
warning *amaran*
wash *cuci, mencuci*
watch (wristwatch) *jam tangan*
watch over, guard *mengawasi, menjaga*
watch, to (a show or movie) *menonton*
watch, look, see *lihat, melihat*
water *air*
water buffalo *kerbau*
waterfall *air terjun*
watermelon *semikai, semangka, tembikai*

wave *ombak*
wax *lilin*
way of, by *melalui*
way, method *cara*
we (excludes the one addressed) *kami*
we (includes the one addressed) *kita*
weak *lemah*
weapon *senjata*
wear, to *pakai, memakai*
weary *penat, lelah*
weather *cuaca*
weave, to *tenun, menenun*
weaving *tenunan*
Wednesday *Rabu*
week *minggu*
weekly *tiap minggu*
weigh, to *timbang*
weight *berat*
welcome, to *sambut, menyambut*
welcome, you're welcome! *sama-sama! kembali!*
well (for water) *perigi*
well, good *baik*
well-cooked, ripe, well-done *masak, matang*
west *barat*
westerner *orang barat*
wet *basah*
what? *apa?*
wheel *roda*
when, at the time *waktu*
when? *bila?*
where to? *ke mana?*
where? *mana?*
while ago *tadi*

while, awhile *sebentar*

while, during *sambil*

white *putih*

who? *siapa?*

whole, all of *seluruh*

whole, to be complete *kesuluruhan*

why? *kenapa?*

wicked *jahat*

wide, width *lebar*

widow *janda*

wife *isteri*

will, shall *hendaklah, akan*

win, to *menang*

wind, breeze *angin*

window *tingkap, jendela*

wine *air anggur*

wing *sayap*

winner *pemenang, juara*

wire *wayar*

with *dengan, sama, beserta*

without *tanpa*

witness *saksi*

witness, to *saksikan, menyaksikan*

woman *perempuan*

wood *kayu*

word *kata*

work on *mengerjakan*

work, occupation *pekerjaan*

work, to function *jalan, berjalan*

work, to *kerja, bekerja*

world *dunia*

worry, to *khuatir, khuatiri*

wrap, to *membungkus*

write, to *tulis, menulis, karang, mengarang*

writer *pengarang*

wrong, false *salah*

Y

yawn *menguap, sangap*

year *tahun*

yell, to *teriak, berteriak*

yellow *kuning*

yes *ya*

yesterday *semalam, kelmarin*

yet, not yet *belum*

you (familiar) *engkau, kamu, awak*

you (formal) *anda, saudara*

you're welcome! *sama-sama, kembali*

young, unripe *muda*

younger brother or sister *adik*

youth (state of being young) *remaja*

youth (young person) *remaja*

Z

zero *kosong*

zoo *kebun binatang*

Bahasa Malaysia–English Dictionary

The following is a list of words commonly used in colloquial, everyday speech. Words borrowed directly from English have generally been omitted since they are readily understood by English speakers.

Verbs are normally listed under their root forms, without prefixes or suffixes. Prefixed and suffixed forms are then given only in cases where they are commonly used, and have more or less the same meaning as the simple root form alone. For more information on verbal affixes and derived forms, see Appendix A.

Nouns derived from simple roots have been listed alphabetically with their respective prefixes and suffixes attached, rather than being listed under the root word. This means you don't have to know what the root is, but can simply look up the affixed form.

A

abang older brother

acara program

ada to be, have, exist

adat custom, tradition, culture

adik younger brother or sister

agak guess, estimate

agama religion

agar in order that, so that

ahli member

air water

air masak boiled water

air minum drinking water

air panas hot spring

air terjun waterfall

ais ice

ajak to ask along, invite

ajar, mengajar to teach

akan shall, will

akar root

akhir last, end

akibat result

aku I (informal)

akui, mengakui to admit, confess

alam nature

alamat address

alat tool, utensil, instrument

aman safe, peaceful

amaran warning

ambil, mengambil to take

ampun forgiveness, mercy

ampuni, mengampuni to forgive

anak child

anak lelaki son

anak perempuan daughter

anak saudara niece/nephew

anda you (formal)

anggota member

anggur grape

angin wind

angkat, mengangkat to lift, raise up

anjing dog

antara among, between

apa khabar? how are you?

apa? what?

api fire

arah direction

asal, berasal origin; to originate

asam sour

asap smoke

asing foreign

asli indigenous, original

asrama hostel

atas above, upstairs

atau or

atur, mengatur to arrange, organize

awas! be careful! look out!

ayah father

ayam chicken

ayuh come on, let's go

B

babi pig

baca, membaca to read

badan body

bagaimana? how?

bagi for, to share

bagus good

bahagi to divide

bahagia happy

bahagian division, part

bahan material, ingredient

bahasa language

bahaya danger, dangerous

bahu shoulder

bahwa that (introduces a quotation or a subordinate clause)

baik good

baju blouse, shirt

bakar, membakar to burn; roasted, toasted (of food)

bakul basket

balas, membalas to answer (a letter), reciprocate

balasan a reply

balik to return, go back

bandar, bandaraya town, city

banding, membandingkan to compare to

bangsa nationality, race

bangun, membangun awaken; to build

bangunan building

banjir flood

bantal pillow

bantu, membantu to help

banyak many, much

bapa father

bapa saudara uncle

barang thing, item

barangkali probably, perhaps

barat west

baru new, just now

bas bus

basah wet

basikal bicycle

batal, membatalkan to cancel

batang stick, pole

batas edge, boundary

batu stone

batuk cough

bau smell, odor (bad)

bawa, membawa to carry

bawah below, under

bawang onion

bawang putih garlic

bayam spinach

bayang shadow

bayangkan, membayangkan to imagine

bayar, membayar to pay

bebas free, unrestrained

beberapa some

beca pedicab

beg bag, baggage

begini thus, so, like this

begitu thus, so, like that

bekerja to work

belajar to study

belakang behind, rear

belanja to shop, expense

belas teen

beli, membeli to buy

belok turn

belum not yet

benang thread

benar true

bendera flag

bengkel workshop

bentuk, membentuk shape; to form

berak to defecate

berangkat to depart

berani brave

berapa? how many? how much?

beras uncooked rice

berat heavy

beratur line up

berdaftar registered (post)

berdiri to stand up

beres solved, arranged, okay

bereskan, membereskan to solve, arrange

berhenti to stop

beri, memberi to give

berikut next, following

berikutnya the next, the following

berita news

berkahwin to be married

berkembang to develop, expand

bersih clean

bersihkan, membersihkan to clean

berubah to change

berus brush

besar big

besarkan, membesarkan to enlarge

besi metal, iron, steel

besok tomorrow

betul true, repaired

betulkan, membetulkan to repair, fix

beza, berbeza to differ; difference; to be different

biar! forget about it!

biarkan, membiarkan to allow, let alone, leave be

biasa usual, regular, normal

bicara, berbicara to speak

biji seed

bikin, membikin to do, make

bila? when?

bilang to say, count

bilik room

bilik mandi bathroom

bilik tidur bedroom

bilion billion

binatang animal

bintang star

biru blue

bodoh stupid

bola ball

boleh to be allowed to, may

bongkar to break apart, unpack, disassemble

borong, memborong to buy up

bosan, membosankan to be bored, boring

buah fruit, piece

buang, membuang to cast out, throw away

buang air besar defecate

buang air kecil urinate

buat, membuat to do, make

bubur porridge

budaya culture

buka, membuka to open

bukan not, none

bukit hill

bukti proof

buktikan, membuktikan to prove

buku book

buku panduan guidebook

bulan month, moon

bumi the earth

bumiputera indigenous person

bunga flower

bungkus, bungkusan to wrap; a package

bunuh, membunuh to kill

bunyi, berbunyi a sound; to make noise

buruk bad, no good

burung bird

busuk rotten

C

cabang branch

cacat defect, handicap

cacian insult

hutan simpan forest reserve

cahaya rays

kacak handsome

cakap to speak

campur mixed; to mix

cantik beautiful (of women)

cap brand

capai, mencapai to reach, attain

cara way

cari, mencari to look for

cat paint

catat, mencatat to note down

catatan notes

catur chess

cawan cup

celaka bad luck, disaster

cemburu jealous

cendawan mushroom, fungus

cepat fast

cerah clear (of weather)

cerai divorced

cerdik clever

cerita story

cermin, mencerminkan
mirror; to reflect

cetak, mencetak to print

cili chilli pepper

cincin ring (jewelry)

cinta, mencintai love; to love

cita-cita goal, ideal

cium, mencium to kiss

coba, mencoba to try, to try on

cocok to fit, be suitable,
match

coklat brown

contoh sample, example

cuaca weather

cuci, mencuci to wash,
develop (of film)

cuka vinegar

cukup enough

cukur to shave

cuma merely

curi, mencuri to steal

curiga to suspect

D

dada chest

daerah region, district

daftar to register; a list

dagang business

daging meat

dalam inside

dalang puppeteer

damai peace

dan and

dana funds

danau lake

dapat, mendapat to get,
reach, attain, find, succeed,
be able to do

dapur kitchen

darah blood

darat, mendarat land; to
land

dari from, of

darjah degrees

daripada than

darurat emergency

dasar basis

datang to arrive, come

datuk grandfather, honorary
title

daun leaf

daya force

debu dust

dekat near

dekati, mendekati to
approach

demam fever

demikian like that

dendeng meat jerky

dengan with

dengar, mendengar to hear

dengarkan, mendengarkan to listen to

depan front, in front

desa village

desak to urge, push

di in, at, on

di atas on top of, above, upstairs

di bawah below, underneath, downstairs

di mana? where?

di- the passive form of verbs

dia he, she, it, him, her

diam, berdiam silent; to be silent

didik, mendidik to educate

dilarang to be forbidden

dingin cool

diri, berdiri self; stand, to stand up

dirikan, mendirikan to build, establish

Disember December

doa prayer

dompet wallet

dorong, mendorong to push

dua two

dua belas twelve

dua puluh twenty

duduk to sit down

duit money (coins)

dulu first, beforehand

dunia world

duta ambassador, emissary

duti kastam customs duty

E

ejen agent

ekor tail

emas gold

empat four

enak tasty

enam six

encer thin (of liquids)

Encik Mister

engkau you

epal apple

erat closely related, connected

erti, bererti meaning, to mean

F

fasih fluent

Februari February

fikir, berfikir to think

fikiran thoughts

G

gabung to join together

gading ivory

gadis girl

gado-gado vegetable salad with peanut sauce

gagah strong, dashing

gagal to fail

gajah elephant

gaji wages, salary

galak fierce

gambar picture, drawing, image

gambarkan, menggambarkan to draw; to describe

ganggu, mengganggu to disturb, bother

gangguan disturbance

ganja marijuana

ganti, menggantikan to change, switch

gantung to hang

garam salt

garis line

garpu fork

gaya style

gayung ladle, dipper

gedung warehouse

gelang bracelet

gelanggang arena

gelap dark

gelaran title, degree

gelas glass

gema echo

gemar to fancy, be a fan of

gembira happy, rejoicing

gemuk fat (of a person)

gerai stall

gerak, bergerak to move

gerakan movement

gereja church

giat active

gigi teeth

gila crazy

goreng fried

gosok to scrub, brush, iron

goyang to swing, shake

gua cave

gugur wilt, fall (of leaves)

gula sugar

gula-gula candy, sweets

gulai spicy sauce

guling to rotate; a bolster pillow

guna, berguna to be useful

guna-guna magical spells

gunakan, menggunakan to make use of

gunting scissors

gunung mountain

gunung api volcano

guru teacher

guruh thunder

H

habis gone, finished

habiskan, menghabiskan to finish off

hadapi, menghadapi to face, confront

hadiah gift, tip

hadir to attend

hairan surprised

hak rights, belongings

hak asasi manusia human rights

halal lawful, permitted

halau chase away

halus fine, refined

hambat, menghambat to hinder

hambatan hindrance

hamil pregnant

hampir almost

hancur crushed

hancurkan, menghancurkan to crush, break

hangat warm

hantar, bimbing, membimbing to guide, lead

hantu ghost

hanya only

harap, berharap to hope

harapkan, mengharapkan to expect

harga cost

hari day, day of the week

hari depan in future

hari ini today

hari jadi birthday

harimau tiger

harus to be necessary, must

hasil, berhasil result; to succeed

hasilkan, menghasilkan to produce

hasrat desire

hati heart, liver

hati-hati! be careful!

haus thirsty

hebat great, formidable

hemat economical

hendak to intend to

henti, berhenti to stop

hidung nose

hidup to live

hijau green

hilang lost

hilangkan, menghilangkan to get rid of

hina, menghina insulted; to insult

hisap, menghisap to inhale

hitam black

hodoh ugly

hormat respect

hubungan contacts

hubungi to contact

hujan rain

hukum law

hutan forest, jungle

hutang debt

I

ia he, she, it (= *dia*)

ibu mother

ikan fish

ikat to tie; handwoven textiles

iklim climate

ikut, mengikuti to follow along, go along

ilmu science

imbang equal

indah beautiful (of things, places)

ingat, beringat to remember

ingatkan, mengingatkan to remind

ini this

intan diamond

inti essence, core, filling

ipar relative by marriage

iri hati envious

isi, mengisi to fill

Isnin Monday

istana palace

istimewa special

isteri wife

istirahat rest

itik duck

itu that

izinkan, mengizinkan to permit

J

jadi, menjadi to become, happen

jadual waktu schedule

jaga, menjaga to guard

jagung corn

jahat wicked

jahit, menjahit to sew

jalan to walk, function; a street or road

jalan-jalan to go out, go walking

jam hour, o'clock

jambatan bridge

jamin, menjamin to guarantee, assure

jaminan a guarantee, assurance

janda widow

jangan do not!

jangka period (of time)

janji, berjanji to promise

jantung heart

jarak distance

jarang rarely, scarce

jari fingers

jaring net

jarum needle

jasa service

jatuh to fall

jatuhkan, menjatuhkan to drop, fall over

jauh far

jawab, menjawab to answer, reply

jawapan an answer

jelas clear

jelaskan, menjelaskan to clarify

jemput, menjemput to invite, to call for

jemur to dry out

jenaka funny

jendela window

jenis type, sort

jenkel annoyed

jika, jikalau if

jiwa soul

jual, menjual to sell

juara champion

judi, berjudi to gamble

judul title, subject

juga also

Jumaat Friday

jumlah amount, total

jumpa, berjumpa, menjumpai to meet

jurusan direction

juta million

K

kabar, khabar news

kaca glass

kacamata eyeglasses

kacang bean, peanut

kacang kapri snowpeas

kacang buncis French (green) beans

kacau confused, messy

kad card

kadang-kadang sometimes

kain cloth

kain cadar sheet

kakak older sister

kaki leg, foot

kaku stiff

kalah to lose, be defeated

kalahkan, mengalahkan to defeat

kalau if

kali times, occurrences

kalimat sentence

kambing lamb, mutton, goat, sheep

kami we

kampung village, hamlet

kamu you (informal)

kamus dictionary

kanan right

kangkung a kind of spinach

kantung pocket

kapal ship

kapas cotton

karang, mengarang later; to write

karangan writings

kerana because

karut nonsense

kasar coarse

kasih to give, love

kasihan pity, sorrow

kasut shoe

kata, berkata word; to say

katil bed

kaunter counter, ticket window

kawan friend

kaya rich; coconut jam

kayu wood

ke to, towards

kebangsaan nationality

kebudayaan culture

kebun garden

kebun binatang zoo

kebun raya botanical gardens

kecelakaan accident

kecil small

kecuali except for

kecut shrunken

kedai shop

kedua second

kegiatan activity

kejam harsh, cruel

kejar, mengejar to chase

keju cheese

kejut, terkejut surprised, startled

kek cake

kelabu (warna) gray

kelambu mosquito net

kelamin a pair

kelapa coconut

kelas class

keliling encircle, to go around

kelilingi, mengelilingi to encircle, go around

kelmarin yesterday

keluar to go out, exit

keluarkan, mengeluarkan to put out, produce

keluarga family

keluh, mengeluh a sigh, to sign, yearn

kemarau dry season, drought

kembali to return

kembang blossom

kembangkan, mengembangkan to expand

kemudian then, afterwards

kena to hit, to suffer

kenal, mengenal to know, to recognize

kenangan memories
kenapa? why?
kencing urinate
kental thick (of liquids)
kentang potato
kentut to fart
kenyang full, having eaten enough
kepada to, toward (a person)
kepala head, leader
kepercayaan beliefs, faith
keputusan decision
kera monkey
kerajaan government
kerajaan, jabatan government department
keramat sacred
keranjang basket
keras hard
kerbau water buffalo
kereta car
keretapi train
keretek clove cigarette
kering dry
keringat sweat
kerja, bekerja work
kertas paper
kerusi chair
kesal regrettable
kesan impression
kesempatan opportunity, chance
ketam crab
ketat strict
ketawa laugh
ketemu to find, meet
keterangan information
ketiga third

ketuk to knock
keyakinan confidence
khabar, kabar news
Khamis Thursday
khidmat, perkhidmatan to serve, service
khuatir to worry about
khusus special
kicap soy sauce
kilang factory
kilat lightning
kini nowadays, presently
kipas fan
kipas angin electric fan
kira bill, account
kira, mengira to calculate, to guess, suppose
kiri left
kirim, mengirim to send
kita we
kobis cabbage
kobis bunga cauliflower
kocek pocket
kolam pool
kolam renang swimming pool
kopi coffee
korban sacrifice, victim
kos cost
kosong empty, zero
kota city, fort
kotak box
kotor dirty
kraftangan handicraft
kuah gravy
kuasa power, authority
kuat strong, energetic
kubu fortress

kuburan gravesite
kucing cat
kuda horse
kuih cake, cookie, pastry
kuku fingernail
kukus steamed
kulit skin, leather
kumis moustache
kumpul gather
kumpulan club, group
kunang-kunang firefly
kunci key, lock
kuning yellow
kuno ancient
kupas, mengupas to peel
kupu-kupu butterfly
kura-kura turtle
kurang less
kurangi, mengurangi to reduce
kurus thin
kutip to collect payment

L

laci drawer
lada chilli pepper
lada hitam black pepper
lagi more
lagu song
-lah! word giving emphasis to sentence or phrase
lahir to be born
lahirkan, melahirkan to give birth
lain different
laju speed

laki-laki male
laku; berlaku valid; to exist, happen
lakukan, melakukan to do
lalu past; then
lalui to pass by
lama old (of things); a long time
lambat slow
lampu light, lamp
lancar smooth, proficient, fluent
langit sky
langkah step, measure
langsung directly, non-stop
lantai floor
lantas then, straight away
lapan eight
lapang spacious, wide
lapangan field
lapar hungry
lapis layer
lapor, melapor to report
laporan report, a report
laporkan, melaporkan to report, to announce
larang, melarang to forbid
lari run, escape
latihan practice
laut sea
lawan opposite; opponent
lawatan visit
layan, melayani to serve (food, etc.)
layar, berlayar a sail; to sail
lebar wide
lebih more
lebih banyak more of

lebih-kurang approximately, about

leher neck

lekat to stick

lelaki man

lelong sale (at reduced prices)

lemah weak

lembu beef, cattle

lembut gentle

lengan arm

lengkap complete

lepas after, past

lesen license

letih weary, tired

letak to place

lewat to pass, overdue

lidah tongue

lidi satay skewer

lihat, melihat to see, look (also observe, visit, or read)

lilin candle, wax

lima five

limau lime, lemon

limpah to overflow, be overflowing

lindungi to protect

lipat, melipat to fold

lobak merah carrot

loket ticket window, counter

lombok chilli pepper

lompat, melompat to jump

lorong lane

luar outside

luar negeri overseas

luas broad, spacious

lubang hole

lucu funny

luka injury, wound

lukis, melukis to paint, to draw

lukisan painting, drawing

lumayan sufficient, enough

lunas paid

lupa to forget; forgotten

lupakan, melupakan to forget about

lurus straight

lusa the day after tomorrow

M

ma'af! sorry!

mabuk drunk

Mac March

macam kind, like (similar to)

macan tiger

madu honey

mahal expensive

main to play

majalah magazine

maju to advance

mak mother (term of address)

mak cik aunt

makam grave

makan to eat

makanan food

maksud, bermaksud meaning, intention; to mean

malam night

malas lazy

malu shy, ashamed

mana where

mandi to bathe

mangkuk bowl

manis sweet

marah angry

mari come, come here

mas gold

masa period

masak to cook

masakan cooking, cuisine

masalah problem

masam sour

masih still

masin salty

masuk to come in, enter

masukkan, memasukkan to put inside

mata eye

matahari sun

matang well-cooked, ripe, well-done

mati to die, to stop functioning

mau to want

me- active verb prefix

meja table

melalui by way of, via

melawat to visit

memang indeed

menang to win

menantu son/daughter-in-law

menara tower

menarik interesting

mendung cloudy

mengerti to understand

meninggal to pass away

meninggalkan to leave behind

mentah raw, uncooked, rare

mentega butter

mentua (*bapak*/*ibu*) father/mother-in-law

menurut according to

merah red

merdeka free

mereka they, them

mesjid mosque

mesti must, surely

mesyuarat meeting

mewah lavish, expensive

mi noodles

mihun rice vermicelli

milik to own

mimpi dream

Minggu Sunday

minggu week

minta to ask for, request

minum to drink

minuman drink

minyak oil

miskin poor

mohon to request

motosikal motorcycle

muat load

muda young, unripe

mudah easy

muka face

mulai to start, begin

mulut mouth

muncul to appear

mundur to back up

mungkin maybe, perhaps

muntah to vomit

murah cheap

musim season

musuh enemy

N

naik to ride, go up, climb
nakal naughty
nama name
nanas pineapple
nanti later, to wait
nanti malam tonight
nanti petang this afternoon
nasi rice
negara country, nation
negeri state
nekad determined
nenek grandmother
ngantuk to be sleepy
nginap, menginap to stay overnight
nikah, menikah marrriage, to get married
nilai price, value
nombor number
nyamuk mosquito
nyanyi, bernyanyi to sing
nyawa life
nyonya Straits Chinese woman

O

Ogos August
oleh by, because of
ombak wave, surf
orang person, human being
orang tua old person, parents
oren orange

P

pada on
padang field, square
paderi priest
padi rice plant
pagar fence, hedge
pagi morning
paha thigh
pahat, memahat chisel, to sculpt
pahit bitter
pajak tax, monopoloy
pajang, memajang to display
pak cik uncle
pakai, memakai to use, wear
pakaian clothing
pakaian dalam underwear
paksa, memaksa to force
paku nail
paling the most
paling-paling at the most
pam pump
panas hot (temperature)
pandai clever, smart
pandang, memandang to view, to consider
pandangan view, opinion
pandu to drive
panggang, memanggang roasted; to roast
panggil, memanggil to call, summon
pangkat rank, status
panjang long, length
panjangkan, memanjangkan to extend

pantai beach

parah bad, serious (of illness, problems, etc.)

pasang, memasang to assemble, switch on

pasar a market

pasar raya supermarket

pasarkan, memasarkan to market

pasir sand

pasti sure, certain

pasukan team

patah broken (of bones, long objects)

pawagam movie theatre

payung umbrella

pecah shattered

pecahkan, memecahkan to shatter, break, solve (a problem)

pedagang businessman

pedas hot (spicy)

pegang, memegang to hold, grasp

pegawai civil servant/official

pejabat office

pekerjaan job, occupation

pelanggan customer

pelaut sailor

pelayan servant

pemandangan panoramic view

pemandu driver

pemerintah government

pemimpin leader

pencuri thief, pickpocket

pendek short

pengarang writer

pengaruh influence

penginapan small hotel, accommodation

peninggalan remains

penjara jail

penjelasan clarification

penting important

penuh full

penuhi, memenuhi to fulfill

penumpang passenger

perabot furniture

perahu boat

perak silver

peran role

perang war

perbezaan difference

percaya to believe, have confidence in

percuma free

perempuan woman

pergi to go, to leave

perigi a well (for water)

periksa, memeriksa to examine, inspect

perintah to command; an order

perjanjian agreement

perkembangan development

perkhidmatan service

perlahan-perlahan slowly

perlihatkan, memperlihat-kan to show

perlu to be necessary

permukaan surface

pernah to have already, have ever

pertama first

pertandingan competition

pertanyaan question

pertunjukan show, performance

perut stomach, belly

pesan, memesan to order (food, etc.), an order

pesawat airplane, telephone extension, instrument

pesta party

peta map

peti crate, box

picit, memicit a massage; to massage

pilih, memilih to choose, select

pilihan choice

pindah, memindah to move

pinjam, meminjam to borrow

pinjamkan, meminjamkan to lend

pintar smart, clever

pintu door

pipi cheek

piring saucer

pisah, memisahkan to separate

pisang banana

pisau knife

pokok tree, bush

pondok hut, shack, booth

potong, memotong to cut; a cut, slice

Puan Madam

puas satisfied

puaskan, memuaskan to satisfy

pukul o'clock

pukul, memukul to strike, beat

pulang to go back

pulau island

puluh ten, multiples of ten

puncak peak, summit

punya, mempunyai to have, to own, belong to

pusat center

pusing to rotate, revolve

putar, berputar to turn around

putih white

putus to break off

putuskan, memutuskan to decide

R

Rabu Wednesday

racun poison

ragu-ragu to be doubtful

rahsia secret

raja king

rajin hardworking, industrious

rakan colleague, workmate

rakyat people

rama-rama butterfly, moth

ramah friendly, open

ramai busy, crowded

rambut hair

rancang, merancangkan to plan, to prepare

rancangan a plan

rantai chain

rapat a meeting; to be close together, intimate

rapi orderly, neat

rasa, merasa feeling, taste, opinion; to feel

rasuah bribe

rata even, level

ratus hundred

raya large, great

rayakan, merayakan to celebrate (a holiday)

rebus to boil

rebut to snatch

rehat, istirehat a rest; to rest

rekreasi recreation

remaja youth

rempah-rempah spices

renang, berenang to swim

rendah low

rendang spiced cooked meat

resep prescription, recipe

resmi official

resmikan, meresmikan to inaugurate, officially open

retak crack, cracked

ribu thousand

ringan light

ringkas concise

roda wheel

rokok, merokok cigarette; to smoke

roman novel

rosak broken, damaged

roti bread

ruang, ruangan room, hall

rugi loss, disadvantage

rugikan, merugikan to cause to lose money; to inflict loss

rukun harmonious

rumah house, home

rumit complicated

rumput grass

rupa appearance

rusa deer

S

saat moment, second

sabar patient

Sabtu Saturday

sabun soap

saderi celery

sahabat friend

saing, saingan to compete; competitor

sains science

saja only

sakit sick; painful

saksi witness

saksikan, menyaksikan to witness

sakti supernatural power

saku pocket

salah wrong, false

salahkan, menyalahkan to fault, to blame

salam greetings

saling mutual

salji snow

sama the same; together with

sama-sama you're welcome

sambal chilli paste

sambil while

sambung, menyambung to connect

sambungan connection (telephone)

sambut, menyambut to receive, to welcome (people)

sampah garbage

sampai to arrive, reach; until

sampan small boat

samping side

sampul envelope

sana there

sangat very, extremely

sanggup to be capable of, willing to take on

sangka to think; to guess

sapu broom

sarang nest

saring a filter; to filter

sarung sarong (wrap-around skirt); cover

sastera literature

satay barbecued meat on skewers

satu one

saudara relative, you (formal)

sawah rice paddy

saya I, me

sayang to be fond of, to love; pity, sorrow

sayap wing

sayur, sayuran vegetables

se- prefix meaning one, the same as

sebab because

sebelah next to

sebelas eleven

sebelum before

sebentar in a moment

seberang across from

sebut, menyebut to say

sedang to be in the middle of

sedap delicious

sedar, menyedari to be conscious, to realize

sederhana modest, simple

sedia available

sediakan, menyediakan to prepare, make ready

sedih sad

sedikit little, not much

segala every, all

segar fresh

segera soon

segi angle, side

sehat healthy

seimbang equal, balanced

sejak since

sejarah history

sejuk cold

sekali once, one time; very

sekarang now

sekejap soon, in a moment

sekolah school

selamat congratulations, safe

Selasa Tuesday

selat straits

selatan south

selendang shoulder cloth, shawl, stole

selenggarakan, menyelenggarakan to organize

selesai finished

selidiki, menyelidiki to study, to research

selimut blanket

selisih discrepancy

selsema, demam a cold, influenza

seluar pants, trousers

seludup to smuggle

seluruh, kesuluruhan entire, whole, complete

semalam yesterday

semangat spirit

semangka watermelon

sembahkan, persembahkan to present

sembahyang to pray

sembilan nine

sembuh cured, recovered

sembunyi to hide; hidden

sembur to spray

sementara temporarily; while

semi to sprout

sempat to have time to

sempit narrow

sempurna pure, perfect; completed

semua all

senang easy, simple

sendiri self, oneself, alone

sendirian by oneself, all alone

seni art

seniman artist

senja dusk

senjata weapon

sentuh, menyentuh to touch

senyum, tersenyum to smile

sepi quiet

sepuluh ten

serba all sorts

sering often

serta, berserta together with

seruling flute

sesuai dengan suited to, appropriate

sesuaikan, menyesuaikan to adapt to

sesudah after

setelah after

setem stamp

setengah half

setia loyal

setiausaha secretary

sewa, menyewa to rent

sewakan, menyewakan to rent out

sia-sia to no avail

siang day time

siap ready

siapa? who?

siapkan to make ready

siaran a broadcast, program

sibuk busy

sifat characteristic

sikap attitude

sikat, menyikat comb; to comb

sila please

simpan, menyimpan to keep, store, to deposit, to leave with someone

simpang, menyimpang to diverge from

simpangan intersection

sinar rays

singgah stop by, visit

singkat concise

sini here

siput shellfish

sisa leftover, remainder

sisi side, flank

situ over there

soal matter, problem

soto spiced soup

sotong squid

stesen station

suami husband

suara voice

suasana atmosphere

suatu a certain

subur fertile

sudah already

sudu spoon

suhu temperature

suka, menyukai to like

sukar difficult

suku tribe, one-quarter

sungai river

sungutan complaint

sungguh really, truly

suntik to inject, vaccinate

sup soup

supaya in order that, so that

surat letter, document

surat khabar newspaper

suruh, menyuruh to instruct, command

susah difficult

susu milk

susul, menyusul to follow behind

sutera silk

syarikat company

T

tadi a while ago

tadi malam last night

tafsir, menafsir interpretation; to interpret

tahan to endure, to last

tauhu to know; soybean curds (tofu)

tahun year, years

tajam sharp

takut to fear, to be afraid

tali rope, string

tali pinggang belt

taman garden

tamat ended

tambah to add, increase

tambang fare

tamu guest

tanah soil, land

tanam to plant

tanaman a plant

tanda sign, indication, symbol

tanda tangan signature

tandas toilet

tangan hand, forearm, wrist

tangga stairs, ladder

tanggap, menanggap to react

tanggapan reaction, response

tanggung guaranteed

tanggungjawab responsibility

tangis, menangis to cry

tangkap, menangkap to grasp, to capture

tanpa without

tantangan challenge

tanya, bertanya to ask

tari, menari to dance

tarian dance

tarik to pull

tarikh date (of the month)

tarif tariff, fare

taruh, menaruh to put, place

tasik lake

tawar, menawar tasteless; to make an offer, to bargain

tebal thick, dense

tebu sugarcane

tegang tense, tight

teh tea

tekan to press; to oppress

tekanan pressure

telaga pond, well

telanjang naked

telinga ear

teliti meticulous

teluk bay

telur egg

teman friend

tembok stone wall

tembus, menembus to pierce, penetrate

tempat place

tempat tidur sleeping place, bed

tempe fermented soybean cakes

tempel, menempel to stick

temu, bertemu, menemui to meet

tenaga power, energy

tenang calm

tengah middle

tengah hari midday, noon

tenggara southeast

tenggelam to submerge; to drown

tengok, menengok to see, visit

tentang concerning

tentangan, bertentangan to be opposed, at odds

tentera army

tentu certain, certainly

tentukan, menentukan to establish

tenun, menenun to weave

tenunan weavings

tepat exact, exactly

tepi edge, fringe

tepung flour

terakhir last

terang light, clear, bright

terbang, menerbang to fly

terbit, menerbitkan published; to publish

tergantung it depends, to depend on

terhadap as regards, regarding, towards

teriak, berteriak to shout

terima to receive

terima kasih thank you

terjadi to happen; happened

terjemah to translate

terjun to plunge, tumble down

terkejut surprised

terlalu too (excessive)

terlambat late

terong eggplant, aubergine

tersembunyi hidden

tertawa to laugh

terus straight ahead; continuous

teruskan, meneruskan to continue

tetap fixed, permanent

tetapi but

tiang post, column

tiap every

tiba to arrive

tiba-tiba suddenly

tidak no, not

tidak mungkin impossible

tidak usah to be not necessary

tidur to sleep

tiga three

tiga belas thirteen

tikar mat

tiket ticket

tikus mouse, rat

tilam mattress

timbang to weigh

timbangan scale

timbangkan, pertimbangkan to consider

timbul, menimbul to appear, emerge from

timun cucumber

timur east

tindak, bertindak to act

tindakan action

tinggal to depart, live, reside, stay

tinggalkan to leave behind

tinggi tall, high

tingkat level, story of a building

tinjau, meninjau to survey

tipis thin

tipu, menipu to deceive, cheat

tiram oysters

tokong Chinese temple

tolak, menolak to push; to refuse; to subtract

tolong, menolong to help, assist; please (request)

tonjol, menonjol to stick out

tonton, menonton to watch (a show), to observe

topeng mask

topi hat

tua old (of persons)

tuak palm wine

tuala towel

Tuan Sir

tuang, menuangkan to pour

tubuh body

tugas job, duty

tugu monument

Tuhan God

tuju, menuju towards

tujuan destination, goal

tujuh seven

tukang craftsman, tradesman

tukar, menukar to exchange

tulang bone

tulis, menulis to write

tumbuh, bertumbuh to grow (larger, up)

tumbuhan growth

tumbuk to pound; to punch

tunda, ditunda to postpone; postponed

tunggal single, sole

tunggu, menunggu to wait, wait for

tunjuk to point out, guide to

tuntut, menuntut to demand

turun to go down, get off

turut to obey

tutup, menutup to close, cover

U

ubah, berubah to change

ubat medicine

ubi kentang potato

ucapkan, menucapkan to express, to say

udang shrimp, prawn

udara air, atmosphere

uji to test

ujian test

ujung tip, point, spit (of land)

ukir, mengukir to carve

ukiran carving, statue

ukur, mengukur to measure

ukuran measurement, size

ulang, mengulangi to repeat

ular snake

ulat caterpillar, worm

umpama example

umpamanya for example

umum general, public

umumnya generally

umur age

undang law

undangan invitation

untuk for

untung profit, luck, benefit

upacara ceremony

urat sinews, tendons; vein

urus to arrange; to manage

urusan task, matter, thing to be done

urut massage

usaha efforts, activities; to attempt

usir, mengusir to chase away, out

utama most important, chief

utara north

W

wah! exclamation of surprise

waktu when; time

wang money

wang tunai cash

wanita lady

warga negara citizen

wap steam

warna color

warta berita news

wartawan journalist

warung eating stall, small restaurant

watak character, personality

wau kite

wayang a show (film), performance

wayang kulit shadow puppet play

wayar wire

wisma house (institution); public building

Y

ya yes

Yahudi Jew

yakin convinced

yang the one who, that which

Yang Di Pertuan Agung Supreme Ruler, King

yayasan foundation

Z

zaman epoch, era, period

zamrud emerald